Washington Irving's New York Short Stories

The Legend of Sleepy Hollow
Rip Van Winkle
Mountjoy

drawings by Diane Janowski

Washington Irving's New York Short Stories
by Washington Irving
Compiled and reprinted by New York History Review
Drawings by Diane Janowski

The Legend of Sleepy Hollow, originally published in *The Sketch Book of Geoffrey Crayon, Gent.*, sixth installment March 15, 1820

Rip Van Winkle, originally published in *The Sketch Book of Geoffrey Crayon, Gent.* first installment June 23, 1819

Mountjoy, originally published in *The Crayon Papers*, 1890

For more information, visit our website NewYorkHistoryReview.com

ISBN-10:0983848769
ISBN-13:978-0-9838487-6-9

Printed in the United States of America

for Kate, Lucy, and Annie

Table of Contents

The Legend of Sleepy Hollow

In the bosom of one of those spacious coves which indent the eastern shore of the Hudson, at that broad expansion of the river denominated by the ancient Dutch navigators the Tappan Zee, and where they always prudently shortened sail and implored the protection of Saint Nicholas, there lies a small market town which is generally known by the name of Tarry Town. This name was given by the good housewives of the adjacent country from the inveterate propensity of their husbands to linger about the village tavern on market days. Not far from this village, perhaps about two miles, there is a little valley among high hills which is one of the quietest places in the whole world. A small brook murmurs through it and, with the occasional whistle of a quail or tapping of a woodpecker, is almost the only sound that ever breaks the uniform tranquillity.

From the listless repose of the place, this sequestered glen has long been known by the name of Sleepy Hollow. Some say that the place was bewitched during the early days of the Dutch settlement; others, that an old Indian chief, the wizard of his tribe, held his powwows there before the country was discovered by Master Hendrick Hudson. Certain it is, the place still continues under the sway of some witching power that holds a spell over the minds of the descendants of the original settlers. They are given to all kinds of marvelous beliefs, are subject to trances and visions, and frequently hear music and voices in the air. The whole neighborhood abounds with local tales, haunted spots, and twilight superstitions.

The dominant spirit that haunts this enchanted region is the apparition of a figure on horseback without a head. It is said to be the ghost of a Hessian trooper, whose head had been carried away by a cannonball in some nameless battle during the Revolutionary War, and who is ever seen by the countryfolk, hurrying along in the gloom of the night as if on the wings of the wind. Historians of those parts allege that the body of the trooper having been buried in the yard of a church at no great distance, the ghost rides forth to the scene of battle in nightly quest of his head; and that the rushing speed with which he sometimes passes along the Hollow is owing to his being in a hurry to get back to the churchyard before daybreak. The specter is known, at all the country firesides, by the name of the Headless Horseman of Sleepy Hollow.

It is remarkable that this visionary propensity is not confined to native inhabitants of this little retired Dutch valley, but is unconsciously imbibed by everyone who resides there for a time. However wide-awake they may have been before they entered that sleepy region, they are sure, in a little time, to inhale the witching influence of the air and begin to grow imaginative, to dream dreams, and see apparitions.

In this by-place of nature there abode, some thirty years since, a worthy wight of the name of Ichabod Crane, a native of Connecticut, who "tarried" in Sleepy Hollow for the purpose of instructing the children of the vicinity. He was tall and exceedingly lank, with narrow shoulders, long arms and legs, hands that dangled a mile out of his sleeves, and feet that might have served for shovels. His head was small, and flat at top, with huge ears, large green glassy eyes, and a long snipe nose, so that it looked like a weathercock perched upon his spindle neck, to tell which way the wind blew. To see him striding along on a windy day, with his clothes bagging and fluttering about him, one might have mistaken him for some scarecrow eloped from a cornfield.

His schoolhouse was a low building of one large room, rudely constructed of logs. It stood in a rather lonely but pleasant situation, just at the foot of a woody hill, with a brook running close by, and a formidable birch tree growing at one end of it. From hence the low murmur of his pupils' voices, conning over their lessons, might be heard on a drowsy summer's day, interrupted now and then by the voice of the master in a tone of menace or command; or by the appalling sound of the birch as he urged some wrongheaded Dutch urchin along the flowery path of knowledge. All this he called "doing his duty," and he never inflicted a chastisement without following it by the assurance, so consolatory to the smarting urchin, that "he would remember it, and thank him for it the longest day he had to live."

When school hours were over, Ichabod was even the companion and playmate of the larger boys; and on holiday afternoons would convoy some of the smaller ones home, who happened to have pretty sisters, or good housewives for mothers, noted for the comforts of the cupboard. Indeed it behooved him to keep on good terms with his pupils. The revenue arising from his school would have been scarcely sufficient to furnish him with daily bread, for he was a huge feeder and, though lank, had the dilating powers of an anaconda. To help out his maintenance he was, according to custom in those parts, boarded and lodged at the homes of his pupils a week at a time; thus going the rounds of the neighborhood, with all his worldly effects tied up in a cotton handkerchief.

That this might not be too onerous for his rustic patrons, he assisted the farmers occasionally by helping to make hay, mending the fences, and driving the cows from pasture. He laid aside, too, all the dominant dignity with which he lorded it in the school, and became wonderfully gentle and ingratiating. He found favor in the eyes of the mothers by petting the children, particularly the youngest, and he would sit with a child on one knee, and rock a cradle with his foot for whole hours together.

In addition to his other vocations, he was the singing master of the neighborhood, and picked up many bright shillings by instructing the young folks in psalmody. Thus, by divers little makeshifts, the worthy pedagogue got on tolerably enough and was thought, by all who understood nothing of the labor of headwork, to have a wonderfully easy life of it.

The schoolmaster is generally a man of some importance in the female circle of a rural neighborhood, being considered a kind of idle, gentlemanlike personage, of vastly superior taste and accomplishments to the rough country swains. How he would figure among the country damsels in the churchyard, between services on Sundays! - gathering grapes for them from the wild vines that overran the surrounding trees; reciting for their amusement all the epitaphs on the tombstones; while the more bashful bumpkins hung sheepishly back, envying his superior elegance and address.

He was, moreover, esteemed by the women as a man of great erudition, for he had read several books quite through, and was a perfect master of Cotton Mather's *History of New England Witchcraft.* His appetite for the marvelous was extraordinary. It was often his delight, after his school was dismissed, to stretch himself on the clover bordering the little brook and there con over old Mather's direful tales in the gathering dusk. Then, as he wended his way to the farmhouse where he happened to be quartered, every sound of nature, the boding cry of the tree toad, the dreary hooting of the screech owl, fluttered his excited imagination. His only resource on such occasions was to sing psalm tunes; and the good people of Sleepy Hollow were often filled with awe at hearing his nasal melody floating along the dusky road.

Another of his sources of fearful pleasure was to pass long winter evenings with the old Dutch wives, as they sat spinning by the fire, with a row of apples roasting and spluttering along the hearth, and listen to their marvelous tales of ghosts and goblins, haunted bridges and haunted houses, and particularly of the headless horseman. But if there was a pleasure in all this

A quaint Dutch house.

while snugly cuddling in the chimney corner, it was dearly purchased by the terrors of his subsequent walk homeward. How often did he shrink with curdling awe at some rushing blast, howling among the trees of a snowy night, in the idea that it was the Galloping Hessian of the Hollow!

All these, however, were mere phantoms of the dark. Daylight put mend to all these evils. He would have passed a pleasant life of it if his path had not been crossed by a being that causes more perplexity to mortal man than ghosts, goblins, and the whole race of witches put together, and that was -- a woman.

Among the musical disciples who assembled, one evening in each week, to receive his instructions in psalmody was Katrina Van Tassel, the only child of a substantial Dutch farmer. She was a blooming lass of fresh eighteen, plump as a partridge, ripe and melting and rosy-cheeked as one of her father's peaches, and universally famed, not merely for her beauty, but her vast expectations. She was withal a little of a coquette, as might be perceived in her dress. She wore ornaments of pure yellow gold to set off her charms, and a provokingly short petticoat to display the prettiest foot and ankle in the country round.

Ichabod Crane had a soft and foolish heart toward the sex; and it is not to be wondered at that so tempting a morsel soon found favor in his eyes, more especially after he had visited her in her paternal mansion. Old Baltus Van Tassel was a perfect picture of a thriving, contented, liberal-hearted farmer. He seldom, it is true, sent either his eyes or his thoughts beyond the boundaries of his own farm; but within those everything was snug, happy, and abundant.

The Van Tassel stronghold was situated on the banks of the Hudson, in one of those green, sheltered, fertile nooks in which the Dutch farmers are so fond of nestling. A great elm tree spread its broad branches over it, at the foot of which bubbled up a spring of the softest and sweetest water. Hard by the farm-house was a vast barn, every window and crevice of which seemed bursting forth with the treasures of the farm. Rows of pigeons were enjoying the sunshine on the roof. Sleek unwieldy porkers were grunting in the repose and abundance of their pens. A stately squadron of snowy geese were riding in an adjoining pond, convoying whole fleets of ducks; regiments of turkeys were gobbling through the farmyard.

The pedagogue's mouth watered as he looked upon this sumptuous promise of luxurious winter fare. In his devouring mind's eye he pictured to himself every roasting pig running about with an apple in his mouth; the pigeons were snugly put to bed in a comfortable pie, and tucked in with a coverlet of crust.

As the enraptured Ichabod fancied all this, and as he rolled his great green eyes over the fat meadowlands, the rich fields of wheat, rye, buckwheat, and Indian corn, and the orchard, burdened with ruddy fruit, which surrounded the warm tenement of Van Tassel, his heart yearned after the damsel who was to inherit these domains, and his imagination expanded with the idea how they might be readily turned into cash, and the money invested in immense tracts of wild land, and shingle palaces in the wilderness. His busy fancy already presented to him the blooming Katrina, with a whole family of children, mounted on the top of a wagon loaded with household trumpery; and he beheld himself bestriding a pacing mare, with a colt at her heels, setting out for Kentucky, Tennessee, or the Lord knows where.

When he entered the house, the conquest of his heart was complete. It was one of those spacious farmhouses, with high-ridged but low-sloping roofs, built in the style handed down from the first Dutch settlers, the projecting eaves forming a piazza along the front. From the piazza the wondering Ichabod entered the hall, which formed the center of the mansion. Here, rows of resplendent pewter, ranged on a long dresser, dazzled his eyes. In one corner stood a huge bag of wool ready to be spun; ears of Indian corn and strings of dried apples and peaches hung in gay festoons along the walls; and a door left ajar gave him a peep into the best parlor, where the claw-footed chairs and dark mahogany tables shone like mirrors. Mock oranges and conch shells decorated the mantelpiece; strings of various colored birds' eggs were suspended above it, and a corner cupboard, knowingly left open, displayed immense treasures of old silver and well-mended china.

From the moment Ichabod laid his eyes upon these regions of delight, the peace of his mind was at an end, and his only study was how to win the heart of the peerless daughter of Van Tassel. In this enterprise, however, he had to encounter a host of rustic admirers, who kept a watchful and angry eye upon each other, but were ready to fly out in the common cause against any new competitor. Among these the most formidable was a burly, roaring, roistering blade of the name of Brom Van Brunt, the hero of the country round, which rang with his feats of strength and hardihood. He was broad-shouldered, with short curly black hair, and a bluff but not unpleasant countenance, having a mingled air of fun and arrogance. From his Herculean frame, he had received the nickname of "Brom Bones." He was famed for great skill in horsemanship; he was foremost at all races and cockfights; and, with the ascendancy which bodily strength acquires in rustic life, was the umpire in all disputes. He was always ready for either a fight or a frolic, but had more mischief and good humor than ill will in his composition. He had three or four boon companions who regarded him as their model, and at the head of whom he scoured the country, attending every scene of feud or merriment for miles round. Sometimes his crew would be heard dashing along past the farmhouses at midnight, with whoop and halloo, and the old dames would exclaim, "Aye, there goes Brom Bones and his gang!"

This hero had for some time singled out the blooming Katrina for the object of his uncouth gallantries; and though his amorous toyings were something like the gentle caresses of a bear, yet it was whispered that she did not altogether discourage his hopes. Certain it is, his advances were signals for rival candidates to retire; insomuch that, when his horse was seen tied to Van Tassel's paling on a Sunday night, all other suitors passed by in despair.

Such was the formidable rival with whom Ichabod Crane had to contend. Considering all things, a stouter man than he would have shrunk from the competition. Ichabod had, however, a happy mixture of pliability and perseverance in his nature; he was in form and spirit like a supplejack - though he bent, he never broke.

To have taken the field openly against his rival would have been madness. Ichabod, therefore, made his advances in a quiet and gently insinuating manner. Under cover of his character of singing master, he had made frequent visits at the farmhouse, carrying on his suit with the daughter by the side of the spring under the great elm, while Balt Van Tassel sat smoking his evening pipe at one end of the piazza and his little wife plied her spinning wheel at the other.

I profess not to know how women's hearts are wooed and won. To me they have always been matters of riddle and admiration. But certain it is that from the moment Ichabod Crane made his advances, the interests of Brom Bones declined; his horse was no longer seen tied at the paiings on Sunday nights, and a deadly feud gradually arose between him and the schoolmaster of Sleepy Hollow. Brom would fain have carried matters to open warfare, and Ichabod had overheard a boast by Bones that he would "double the schoolmaster up, and lay him on a shelf of his own schoolhouse"; but Ichabod was too wary to give him an opportunity. Brom had no alternative but to play off boorish practical jokes upon his rival. Bones and his gang of rough riders smoked out Ichabod's singing school by stopping up the chimney; broke into the schoolhouse at night and turned everything topsy-turvy. But what was still more annoying, Brom took opportunities of turning him to ridicule in presence of his mistress, and had a scoundrel dog whom he taught to whine in the most ludicrous manner, and introduced as a rival of Ichabod's to instruct Katrina in psalmody.

In this way matters went on for some time. On a fine autumnal afternoon, Ichabod, in pensive mood, sat enthroned on the lofty stool whence he usually watched all the concerns of his little schoolroom. His scholars were all busily intent upon their books, or slyly whispering behind them with one eye kept upon the master; and a kind of buzzing stillness reigned. It was suddenly interrupted by the appearance of a Negro, mounted on the back of a ragged colt. He came clattering up to the school door with an invitation to Ichabod to attend a merrymaking to be held that evening at Mynheer Van Tassel's.

Allwas now bustle and hubbub in the lately quiet schoolroom. The scholars were hurried through their lessons, without stopping at trifles; those who were tardy had a smart application now and then in the rear to quicken their speed, and the whole school was turned loose an hour before the usual time.

The gallant Ichabod now spent at least an extra half hour at his toilet, brushing and furbishing up his only suit, of rusty black. That he might make his appearance in the true style ofa cavalier, he borrowed a horse from the farmer with whom he was staying. The animal was a broken-down plow horse that had outlived almost everything but his viciousness. He was gaunt and shaggy, with a ewe neck and a head like a hammer; his rusty mane and tail were tangled and knotted with burrs; one eye had lost its pupil, and was glaring and spectral, but the other had the gleam of a genuine devil. In his day he must have had fire and mettle, if we may judge from the name he bore of Gunpowder.

Ichabod was a suitable figure for such a steed. He rode with short stirrups, which brought his knees nearly up to the pommel of the saddle; his sharp elbows stuck out like grasshoppers'; he carried his whip perpendicularly in his hand, like a scepter, and, as his horse jogged on, the motion of his arms was not unlike the flapping of a pair of wings. A small wool hat rested nearly on the top of his nose, and the skirts of his black coat fluttered out almost to the horse's tail.

Around him nature wore that rich and golden livery which we always associate with the idea of abundance. As he jogged slowly on his way, his eye ranged with delight over the treasures of jolly autumn. On all sides he beheld vast stores of apples gathered into baskets and barrels for the market, others heaped up in rich piles for the cider press. Farther on he beheld great fields of Indian corn, and the yellow pumpkins lying beneath them, turning up their fair round bellies to the sun. He passed the fragrant buckwheat fields, and as he beheld them, soft anticipations stole over his mind of dainty slapjacks, well buttered and garnished with honey by the delicate little dimpled hand of Katrina Van Tassel. It was toward evening that Ichabod arrived at the castle of the Eleer Van Tassel, which he found thronged with the pride and flower of the adjacent country. Old farmers, a spare leathern-faced race, in homespun coats and breeches, blue stockings, huge shoes, and magnificent pewter buckles. Their brisk withered little dames, in close crimped caps, longwaisted short gowns, homespun petticoats, and gay calico pockets hanging on the outside. Buxom lasses, almost as antiquated in dress as their mothers, excepting where a straw hat, a fine ribbon, or perhaps a white frock gave symptoms of city innovation. The sons, in short square-skirted coats with rows of stupendous brass buttons, and their hair generally queued with an eelskin in the fashion of the times, eelskins being esteemed as a potent nourisher and strengthener of the hair. Brom Bones, however, was the hero of the scene, having come to the gathering on his favorite steed, Daredevil, a creature, like himself, full of mettle and mischief, and which no one but himself could manage.

Ichabod was a kind and thankful creature, whose spirits rose with eating as some men's do with drink. He could not help rolling his large eyes round him on the ample charms of a genuine Dutch country tea table in the sumptuous time of autumn. Such heaped-up platters of cakes and crullers of various kinds, known only to experienced Dutch housewives! And then there were apple pies and peach pies and pumpkin pies, besides slices of ham and smoked beef; and, moreover, delectable dishes of preserved plums, and peaches, and pears, and quinces, not to mention broiled shad and roasted chickens; together with bowls of milk and cream, with the motherly teapot sending up its clouds of vapor from the midst. Ichabod chuckled with the possibility that he might one day be lord of all this scene of almost unimaginable luxury and splendor. Then, he thought, how soon he'd turn his back upon the old schoolhouse and snap his fingers in the face of every niggardly patron!

And now the sound of the music from the hall summoned to the dance. The musician was an old gray-headed Negro, who had been the itinerant orchestra of the neighborhood for more than half a century. His instrument was as old and battered as himself. He accompanied every movement of the bow with a motion of the head, bowing almost to the ground and stamping with his foot whenever a fresh couple were to start.

Ichabod prided himself upon his dancing as much as upon his vocal powers. Not a limb, not a fiber about him was idle as his loosely hung frame in full motion went clattering about the room. How could the flogger of urchins be otherwise than animated and joyous! The lady of his heart was his partner in the dance, and smiling graciously in reply to all his amorous oglings; while Brom Bones, sorely smitten with love and jealousy, sat brooding by himself in one corner.

When the dance was at an end, Ichabod was attracted to a knot of the sager folks, who, with old Van Tassel, sat smoking at one end of the piazza, gossiping over former times, and drawing out long stories about ghosts and apparitions, mourning cries and wailings, seen and heard in the neighborhood. Some mention was made of the woman in white, who haunted the dark glen at Raven Rock, and was often heard to shriek on winter nights before a storm, having perished there in the snow. The chief part of the stories, however, turned upon the favorite specter of Sleepy Hollow, the Headless Horseman, who had been heard several times of late near the bridge that crossed the brook in the woody dell next to the church; and, it was said, tethered his horse nightly among the graves in the churchyard.

The tale was told of old Brouwer, a most heretical disbeliever in ghosts, how he met the horseman returning from his foray into Sleepy Hollow, and was obliged to get up behind him; how they galloped over hill and swamp until they reached the church bridge. There the horseman suddenly turned into a skeleton, threw old Brouwer into the brook, and sprang away over the treetops with a clap of thunder.

This story was matched by Brom Bones, who made light of the Galloping Hessian as an arrant jockey. He affirmed that, on returning one night from a neighboring village, he had been overtaken by this midnight trooper; that he had offered to race with him for a bowl of punch, and should have won it, too; but just as they came to the church bridge, the Hessian bolted, and vanished in a flash of fire.

The revel now gradually broke up. The old farmers gathered together their families in their wagons, and were heard for some time rattling along over the distant hills. Some of the damsels mounted behind their favorite swains, and their lighthearted laughter, mingling with the clatter of hoofs, echoed along the silent woodlands. Ichabod only lingered behind, according to the custom of country lovers, to have a tete-a-tete with the heiress, fully convinced that he was now on the highroad to success. Something, however, I fear me, must have gone wrong, for he sallied forth, after no very great interval, with an air quite desolate and chopfallen. Oh, these women! these women! Was Katrina's encouragement of the poor pedagogue all a mere trick to secure her conquest of his rival! Let it suffice to say, Ichabod stole forth with the air of one who had been sacking a henroost, rather than a fair lady's heart. Without looking to the right or left, he went straight to the stable, and with several hearty cuffs and kicks, roused his steed most uncourteously.

It was the very witching time of night that Ichabod, heavy-hearted and crestfallen, pursued his travel homeward. Far below, the Tappan Zee spread its dusky waters. In the dead hush of midnight he could hear the faint barking of a watchdog from the opposite shore. The night grew darker and darker; the stars seemed to sink deeper in the sky, and driving clouds occasionally hid them from his sight. He had never felt so lonely and dismal.

All the stories of ghosts and goblins that he had heard earlier now came crowding upon his recollection. He would, moreover, soon be approaching the very place where many of the scenes of the ghost stories had been laid.

Just ahead, where a small brook crossed the road, a few rough logs lying side by side served for a bridge. A group of oaks and chestnuts, matted thick with wild grapevines, threw a cavernous gloom over it. Ichabod gave Gunpowder half a score of kicks in his starveling ribs,

A Catskill bridge.

and attempted to dash briskly across the bridge; but instead of starting forward, the perverse old animal only plunged to the opposite side of the road into a thicket of brambles. He came to a stand just by the bridge, with a suddenness that nearly sent his rider sprawling over his head. Just at this moment, in the dark shadow on the margin of the brook, Ichabod beheld something huge, misshapen, black, and towering. It stirred not, but seemed gathered up in the gloom, like some gigantic monster ready to spring upon the traveler.

The hair of the affrighted schoolteacher rose upon his head, but, summoning up a show of courage, he demanded in stammering accents, "Who are you!" He received no reply. He repeated his demand in a still more agitated voice. Still there was no answer. Once more he cudgeled the sides of the inflexible Gunpowder and, shutting his eyes, broke forth with involuntary fervor into a psalm tune. Just then the shadowy object of alarm put itself in motion and, with a scramble and a bound, stood at once in the middle of the road. He appeared to be a horseman of large dimensions, and mounted on a black horse of powerful frame. He kept aloof on one side of the road, jogging along on the blind side of old Gunpowder, who had now got over his waywardness.

Ichabod quickened his steed, in hopes of leaving this midnight companion behind. The stranger, however, quickened his horse to an equal pace. Ichabod pulled up, and fell into a walk, thinking to lag behind - the other did the same. His heart began to sink within him. There was something in the stranger's moody silence that was appalling. It was soon fearfully accounted for. On mounting a rising ground, which brought the figure of his fellow traveler in relief against the sky, gigantic in height, and muffled in a cloak, Ichabod was horrorstruck on perceiving that he was headless! But his horror was still more increased on observing that the stranger's head was carried before him on the pommel of the saddle.

Ichabod's terror rose to desperation; he rained a shower of kicks and blows upon Gunpowder, hoping to give his companion the slip, but the specter started full jump with him. Away then they dashed, stones flying and sparks flashing at every bound. Ichabod's flimsy garments fluttered in the air, as he stretched his long lank body away over his horse's head in the eagerness of his flight.

They had now reached that stretch of the road which descends to Sleepy Hollow, shaded by trees for about a quarter of a mile, where it crosses the famous church bridge just before the green knoll on which stands the church.

Gunpowder, who seemed possessed with a demon, plunged headlong downhill. As yet his panic had given his unskillful rider an apparent advantage in the chase; but just as he had got halfway through the hollow, the girths of the saddle gave way, and Ichabod felt it slipping from under him. He had just time to save himself by clasping old Gunpowder round the neck when the saddle fell to the earth. He had much ado to maintain his seat, sometimes slipping on one side, sometimes on another, and sometimes jolted on the high ridge of his horse's backbone, with a violence that he feared would cleave him asunder.

An opening in the trees now cheered him with the hopes that the church bridge was at hand. He saw the whitewashed walls of the church dimly glaring under the trees beyond. He recollected the place where Brom Bones's ghostly competitor had disappeared. "If I can but reach that bridge," thought Ichabod, "I am safe." Just then he heard the black steed panting and blowing close behind him; he even fancied that he felt his hot breath. Another convuisive kick in the ribs, and old Gunpowder sprang upon the bridge; he thundered over the resounding planks; he gained the opposite side; and now Ichabod cast a look behind to see if his pursuer should vanish, according to rule, in a flash of fire and brimstone. Just then he saw the goblin rising in his stirrups, in the very act of hurling his head at him. Ichabod endeavored to dodge the horrible missile, but too late. It encountered his cranium with a tremendous crash - he was tumbled headlong into the dust, and Gunpowder, the black steed, and the goblin rider passed by like a whirlwind.

The next morning old Gunpowder was found without his saddle, and with the bridle under his feet, soberly cropping the grass at his master's gate. Ichabod did not make his appearance at breakfast; dinner hour came, but no Ichabod. The boys assembled at the schoolhouse, and strolled idly about the banks of the brook; but no schoolmaster. An inquiry was set on foot, and after diligent investigation they came upon the saddle trampled in the dirt. The tracks of horses' hoofs deeply dented in the road were traced to the bridge, beyond which, on the bank of a broad part of the brook, was found the hat of the unfortunate Ichabod, and close beside it a shattered pumpkin. The brook was searched, but the body of the schoolmaster was not to be discovered.

The mysterious event caused much speculation at the church on the following Sunday. Knots of gazers were collected in the churchyard, at the bridge, and at the spot where the hat and pumpkin had been found. They shook their heads, and came to the conclusion that Ichabod had been carried off by the Galloping Hessian. As he was a bachelor, and in nobody's debt, nobody troubled his head anymore about him. It is true, an old farmer who had been down to New York on a visit several years after brought home the intelligence that Ichabod Crane was still alive; that he had only changed his quarters to a distant part of the country, had kept school and studied law at the same time, had turned politician, and finally had been made a justice of the Ten Pound Court. Brom Bones too, who shortly after his rival's disappearance conducted the blooming Katrina to the altar, was observed to look exceedingly knowing whenever the story of Ichabod was related, and always burst into a hearty laugh at the mention of the pumpkin, which led some to suspect that he knew more about the matter than he chose to tell.

The old country wives, however, who are the best judges of these matters, maintain to this day that Ichabod was spirited away by supernatural means. The bridge became more than ever an object of superstitious awe, and that may be the reason why the road has been altered of late years, so as to approach the church by the border of the millpond. The schoolhouse, being deserted, soon fell to decay, and was reported to be haunted by the the ghost of the unfortunate teacher; and the plowboy, loitering homeward of a still summer evening, has often fancied Ichabod's voice at a distance, chanting a melancholy psalm tune among the tranquil solitudes of Sleepy Hollow.

Rip Van Winkle

A Posthumous Writing of Diedrich Knickerbocker
By Woden, God of Saxons,
From whence comes Wensday, that is Wodensday,
Truth is a thing that ever I will keep
Unto thylke day in which I creep into
My sepulchre.
CARTWRIGHT

The following Tale was found among the papers of the late Diedrich Knickerbocker, an old gentleman of New York, who was very curious in the Dutch history of the province, and the manners of the descendants from its primitive settlers. His historical researches, however, did not lie so much among books as among men; for the former are lamentably scanty on his favorite topics; whereas he found the old burghers, and still more their wives, rich in that legendary lore, so invaluable to true history. Whenever, therefore, he happened upon a genuine Dutch family, snugly shut up in its low-roofed farmhouse, under a spreading sycamore, he looked upon it as a little clasped volume of black-letter, and studied it with the zeal of a book-worm.

A Catskill view.

The result of all these researches was a history of the province during the reign of the Dutch governors, which he published some years since. There have been various opinions as to the literary character of his work, and, to tell the truth, it is not a whit better than it should be. Its chief merit is its scrupulous accuracy, which indeed was a little questioned on its first appearance, but has since been completely established; and it is now admitted into all historical collections, as a book of unquestionable authority.

The old gentleman died shortly after the publication of his work, and now that he is dead and gone, it cannot do much harm to his memory to say that his time might have been better employed in weightier labors. He, however, was apt to ride his hobby his own way; and though it did now and then kick up the dust a little in the eyes of his neighbors, and grieve the spirit of some friends, for whom he felt the truest deference and affection; yet his errors and follies are remembered "more in sorrow than in anger," and it begins to be suspected, that he never intended to injure or offend. But however his memory may be appreciated by critics, it is still held dear by many folks, whose good opinion is well worth having; particularly by certain biscuit-bakers, who have gone so far as to imprint his likeness on their new-year cakes; and have thus given him a chance for immortality, almost equal to the being stamped on a Waterloo Medal, or a Queen Anne's Farthing.

Whoever has made a voyage up the Hudson must remember the Kaatskill mountains. They are a dismembered branch of the great Appalachian family, and are seen away to the west of the river, swelling up to a noble height, and lording it over the surrounding country. Every change of season, every change of weather, indeed, every hour of the day, produces some change in the magical hues and shapes of these mountains, and they are regarded by all the good wives, far and near, as perfect barometers. When the weather is fair and settled, they are clothed in blue and purple, and print their bold outlines on the clear evening sky, but, sometimes, when the rest of the landscape is cloudless, they will gather a hood of gray vapors about their summits, which, in the last rays of the setting sun, will glow and light up like a crown of glory.

At the foot of these fairy mountains, the voyager may have descried the light smoke curling up from a village, whose shingle-roofs gleam among the trees, just where the blue tints of the upland melt away into the fresh green of the nearer landscape. It is a little village of great antiquity, having been founded by some of the Dutch colonists, in the early times of the province, just about the beginning of the government of the good Peter Stuyvesant, (may he rest in peace!) and there were some of the houses of the original settlers standing within a few years, built of small yellow bricks brought from Holland, having latticed windows and gable fronts, surmounted with weather-cocks.

In that same village, and in one of these very houses (which, to tell the precise truth, was sadly time-worn and weather-beaten), there lived many years since, while the country was yet a province of Great Britain, a simple good-natured fellow of the name of Rip Van Winkle. He was a descendant of the Van Winkles who figured so gallantly in the chivalrous days of Peter Stuyvesant, and accompanied him to the siege of Fort Christina. He inherited, however, but little of the martial character of his ancestors. I have observed that he was a simple good-natured man; he was, moreover, a kind neighbor, and an obedient hen-pecked husband. Indeed, to the latter circumstance might be owing that meekness of spirit which gained him such universal popularity; for those men are most apt to be obsequious and conciliating abroad, who are under the discipline of shrews at home. Their tempers, doubtless, are rendered pliant and malleable in the fiery furnace of domestic tribulation; and a curtain lecture is worth all the sermons in the world for teaching the virtues of patience and long-suffering. A termagant wife may, therefore, in some respects, be considered a tolerable blessing; and if so, Rip Van Winkle was thrice blessed.

Certain it is, that he was a great favorite among all the good wives of the village, who, as usual, with the amiable sex, took his part in all family squabbles; and never failed, whenever they talked those matters over in their evening gossipings, to lay all the blame on Dame Van Winkle. The children of the village, too, would shout with joy whenever he approached. He assisted at their sports, made their playthings, taught them to fly kites and shoot marbles, and told them long stories of ghosts, witches, and Indians. Whenever he went dodging about the village, he was surrounded by a troop of them, hanging on his skirts, clambering on his back, and playing a thousand tricks on him with impunity; and not a dog would bark at him throughout the neighborhood.

The great error in Rip's composition was an insuperable aversion to all kinds of profitable labor. It could not be from the want of assiduity or perseverance; for he would sit on a wet rock, with a rod as long and heavy as a Tartar's lance, and fish all day without a murmur, even though he should not be encouraged by a single nibble. He would carry a fowling-piece on his shoulder for hours together, trudging through woods and swamps, and up hill and down dale, to shoot a few squirrels or wild pigeons. He would never refuse to assist a neighbor even in the roughest toil, and was a foremost man at all country frolics for husking Indian corn, or building stone-fences; the women of the village, too, used to employ him to run their errands, and to do such little odd jobs as their less obliging husbands would not do for them. In a word Rip was ready to attend to anybody's business but his own; but as to doing family duty, and keeping his farm in order, he found it impossible.

In fact, he declared it was of no use to work on his farm; it was the most pestilent little piece of ground in the whole country; every thing about it went wrong, and would go wrong, in spite of him. His fences were continually falling to pieces; his cow would either go astray, or get among the cabbages; weeds were sure to grow quicker in his fields than anywhere else; the rain always made a point of setting in just as he had some out-door work to do; so that though his patrimonial estate had dwindled away under his management, acre by acre, until there was little more left than a mere patch of Indian corn and potatoes, yet it was the worst conditioned farm in the neighborhood.

His children, too, were as ragged and wild as if they belonged to nobody. His son Rip, an urchin begotten in his own likeness, promised to inherit the habits, with the old clothes of his father. He was generally seen trooping like a colt at his mother's heels, equipped in a pair of his father's cast-off galligaskins, which he had much ado to hold up with one hand, as a fine lady does her train in bad weather.

Rip Van Winkle, however, was one of those happy mortals, of foolish, well-oiled dispositions, who take the world easy, eat white bread or brown, whichever can be got with least thought or trouble, and would rather starve on a penny than work for a pound. If left to himself, he would have whistled life away in perfect contentment; but his wife kept continually dinning in his ears about his idleness, his carelessness, and the ruin he was bringing on his family. Morning, noon, and night, her tongue was incessantly going, and everything he said or did was sure to produce a torrent of household eloquence. Rip had but one way of replying to all lectures of the kind, and that, by frequent use, had grown into a habit. He shrugged his shoulders, shook his head, cast up his eyes, but said nothing. This, however, always provoked a fresh volley from his wife; so that he was fain to draw off his forces, and take to the outside of the house - the only side which, in truth, belongs to a hen-pecked husband.

Rip's sole domestic adherent was his dog Wolf, who was as much hen-pecked as his master; for Dame Van Winkle regarded them as companions in idleness, and even looked upon Wolf with an evil eye, as the cause of his master's going so often astray. True it is, in all points of spirit befitting an honorable dog, he was as courageous an animal as ever scoured the woods - but what courage can withstand the ever-during and all-besetting terrors of a woman's tongue? The moment Wolf entered the house his crest fell, his tail drooped to the ground, or curled between his legs, he sneaked about with a gallows air, casting many a sidelong glance at Dame Van Winkle, and at the least flourish of a broom-stick or ladle, he would fly to the door with yelping precipitation.

Times grew worse and worse with Rip Van Winkle as years of matrimony rolled on; a tart temper never mellows with age, and a sharp tongue is the only edged tool that grows keener with constant use. For a long while he used to console himself, when driven from home, by frequenting a kind of perpetual club of the sages, philosophers, and other idle personages of the village; which held its sessions on a bench before a small inn, designated by a rubicund portrait of His Majesty George the Third. Here they used to sit in the shade through a long lazy summer's day, talking listlessly over village gossip, or telling endless sleepy stories about nothing. But it would have been worth any statesman's money to have heard the profound discussions that sometimes took place, when by chance an old newspaper fell into their hands from some passing traveller. How solemnly they would listen to the contents, as drawled out by Derrick Van Bummel, the schoolmaster, a dapper learned little man, who was not to be daunted by the most gigantic word in the dictionary; and how sagely they would deliberate upon public events some months after they had taken place.

The opinions of this junto were completely controlled by Nicholas Vedder, a patriarch of the village, and landlord of the inn, at the door of which he took his seat from morning till night, just moving sufficiently to avoid the sun and keep in the shade of a large tree; so that the neighbors could tell the hour by his movements as accurately as by a sundial. It is true he was rarely heard to speak, but smoked his pipe incessantly. His adherents, however (for every great man has his adherents), perfectly understood him, and knew how to gather his opinions. When anything that was read or related displeased him, he was observed to smoke his pipe vehemently, and to send forth short, frequent and angry puffs; but when pleased, he would inhale the smoke slowly and tranquilly, and emit it in light and placid clouds; and sometimes, taking the pipe from his mouth, and letting the fragrant vapor curl about his nose, would gravely nod his head in token of perfect approbation.

From even this stronghold the unlucky Rip was at length routed by his termagant wife, who would suddenly break in upon the tranquillity of the assemblage and call the members all to naught; nor was that august personage, Nicholas Vedder himself, sacred from the daring tongue of this terrible virago, who charged him outright with encouraging her husband in habits of idleness.

Poor Rip was at last reduced almost to despair; and his only alternative, to escape from the labor of the farm and clamor of his wife, was to take gun in hand and stroll away into the woods. Here he would sometimes seat himself at the foot of a tree, and share the contents of his wallet with Wolf, with whom he sympathized as a fellow-sufferer in persecution. "Poor Wolf," he would say, "thy mistress leads thee a dog's life of it; but never mind, my lad, whilst I live thou shalt never want a friend to stand by thee!" Wolf would wag his tail, look wistfuly in his master's face, and if dogs can feel pity I verily believe he reciprocated the sentiment with all his heart.

In a long ramble of the kind on a fine autumnal day, Rip had unconsciously scrambled to one of the highest parts of the Kaatskill mountains. He was after his favorite sport of squirrel shooting, and the still solitudes had echoed and re-echoed with the reports of his gun. Panting and fatigued, he threw himself, late in the afternoon, on a green knoll, covered with mountain herbage, that crowned the brow of a precipice. From an opening between the trees he could overlook all the lower country for many a mile of rich woodland. He saw at a distance the lordly Hudson, far, far below him, moving on its silent but majestic course, with the reflection of a purple cloud, or the sail of a lagging bark, here and there sleeping on its glassy bosom, and at last losing itself in the blue highlands.

On the other side he looked down into a deep mountain glen, wild, lonely, and shagged, the bottom filled with fragments from the impending cliffs, and scarcely lighted by the reflected rays of the setting sun.

Poor Wolf.

For some time Rip lay musing on this scene; evening was gradually advancing; the mountains began to throw their long blue shadows over the valleys; he saw that it would be dark long before he could reach the village, and he heaved a heavy sigh when he thought of encountering the terrors of Dame Van Winkle.

As he was about to descend, he heard a voice from a distance, hallooing, "Rip Van Winkle! Rip Van Winkle!" He looked round, but could see nothing but a crow winging its solitary flight across the mountain. He thought his fancy must have deceived him, and turned again to descend, when he heard the same cry ring through the still evening air: "Rip Van Winkle! Rip Van Winkle!" - at the same time Wolf bristled up his back, and giving a low growl, skulked to his master's side, looking fearfully down into the glen. Rip now felt a vague apprehension stealing over him; he looked anxiously in the same direction, and perceived a strange figure slowly toiling up the rocks, and bending under the weight of something he carried on his back. He was surprised to see any human being in this lonely and unfrequented place, but supposing it to be some one of the neighborhood in need of his assistance, he hastened down to yield it.

On nearer approach he was still more surprised at the singularity of the stranger's appearance. He was a short square-built old fellow, with thick bushy hair, and a grizzled beard. His dress was of the antique Dutch fashion - a cloth jerkin strapped round the waist - several pair of breeches, the outer one of ample volume, decorated with rows of buttons down the sides, and bunches at the knees. He bore on his shoulder a stout keg, that seemed full of liquor, and made signs for Rip to approach and assist him with the load. Though rather shy and distrustful of this new acquaintance, Rip complied with his usual alacrity; and mutually relieving one another, they clambered up a narrow gully, apparently the dry bed of a mountain torrent. As they ascended, Rip every now and then heard long rolling peals, like distant thunder, that seemed to issue out of a deep ravine, or rather cleft, between lofty rocks, toward which their rugged path conducted. He paused for an instant, but supposing it to be the muttering of one of those transient thunder-showers which often take place in mountain heights, he proceeded. Passing through the ravine, they came to a hollow, like a small amphitheatre, surrounded by perpendicular precipices, over the brinks of which impending trees shot their branches, so that you only caught glimpses of the azure sky and the bright evening cloud. During the whole time Rip and his companion had labored on in silence; for though the former marvelled greatly what could be the object of carrying a keg of liquor up this wild mountain, yet there was something strange and incomprehensible about the unknown, that inspired awe and checked familiarity.

On entering the amphitheatre, new objects of wonder presented themselves. On a level spot in the centre was a company of odd-looking personages playing at nine-pins. They were dressed in a quaint outlandish fashion; some wore short doublets, others jerkins, with long knives in their belts, and most of them had enormous breeches, of similar style with that of the guide's. Their visages, too, were peculiar: one had a large beard, broad face, and small piggish eyes: the face of another seemed to consist entirely of nose, and was surmounted by a white sugar-loaf hat set off with a little red cock's tail. They all had beards, of various shapes and colors. There was one who seemed to be the commander. He was a stout old gentleman, with a weather-beaten countenance; he wore a laced doublet, broad belt and hanger, high-crowned hat and feather, red stockings, and high-heeled shoes, with roses in them. The whole group reminded Rip of the figures in an old Flemish painting, in the parlor of Dominie Van Shaick, the village parson, and which had been brought over from Holland at the time of the settlement.

What seemed particularly odd to Rip was, that though these folks were evidently amusing themselves, yet they maintained the gravest faces, the most mysterious silence, and were, withal, the most melancholy party of pleasure he had ever witnessed. Nothing interrupted the stillness of the scene but the noise of the balls, which, whenever they were rolled, echoed along the mountains like rumbling peals of thunder.

As Rip and his companion approached them, they suddenly desisted from their play, and stared at him with such fixed statue-like gaze, and such strange, uncouth, lack-lustre countenances, that his heart turned within him, and his knees smote together. His companion now emptied the contents of the keg into large flagons, and made signs to him to wait upon the company. He obeyed with fear and trembling; they quaffed the liquor in profound silence, and then returned to their game.

By degrees Rip's awe and apprehension subsided. He even ventured, when no eye was fixed upon him, to taste the beverage, which he found had much of the flavor of excellent Hollands. He was naturally a thirsty soul, and was soon tempted to repeat the draught. One taste provoked another; and he reiterated his visits to the flagon so often that at length his senses were overpowered, his eyes swam in his head, his head gradually declined, and he fell into a deep sleep.

On waking, he found himself on the green knoll whence he had first seen the old man of the glen. He rubbed his eyes - it was a bright sunny morning. The birds were hopping and twittering among the bushes, and the eagle was wheeling aloft, and breasting the pure mountain breeze. "Surely," thought Rip, "I have not slept here all night." He recalled the occurrences before he fell asleep. The strange man with a keg of liquor - the mountain ravine - the wild retreat among the rocks - the woe-begone party at ninepins - the flagon - "Oh! that flagon! that wicked flagon!" thought Rip - "what excuse shall I make to Dame Van Winkle!"

He looked round for his gun, but in place of the clean well-oiled fowling-piece, he found an old firelock lying by him, the barrel incrusted with rust, the lock falling off, and the stock worm-eaten. He now suspected that the grave roysterers of the mountain had put a trick upon him, and having dosed him with liquor, had robbed him of his gun. Wolf, too, had disappeared, but he might have strayed away after a squirrel or partridge.

He whistled after him and shouted his name, but all in vain; the echoes repeated his whistle and shout, but no dog was to be seen.

He determined to revisit the scene of the last evening's gambol, and if he met with any of the party, to demand his dog and gun. As he rose to walk, he found himself stiff in the joints, and wanting in his usual activity. "These mountain beds do not agree with me," thought Rip; "and if this frolic should lay me up with a fit of the rheumatism, I shall have a blessed time with Dame Van Winkle." With some difficulty he got down into the glen: he found the gully up which he and his companion had ascended the preceding evening; but to his astonishment a mountain stream was now foaming down it, leaping from rock to rock, and filling the glen with babbling murmurs. He, however, made shift to scramble up its sides, working his toilsome way through thickets of birch, sassafras, and witch-hazel, and sometimes tripped up or entangled by the wild grapevines that twisted their coils or tendrils from tree to tree, and spread a kind of network in his path.

At length he reached to where the ravine had opened through the cliffs to the amphitheatre; but no traces of such opening remained. The rocks presented a high impenetrable wall over which the torrent came tumbling in a sheet of feathery foam, and fell into a broad deep basin, black from the shadows of the surrounding forest. Here, then, poor Rip was brought to a stand. He again called and whistled after his dog; he was only answered by the cawing of a flock of idle crows, sporting high in air about a dry tree that overhung a sunny precipice; and who, secure in their elevation, seemed to look down and scoff at the poor man's perplexities. What was to be done? the morning was passing away, and Rip felt famished for want of his breakfast. He grieved to give up his dog and gun; he dreaded to meet his wife; but it would not do to starve among the mountains. He shook his head, shouldered the rusty firelock, and, with a heart full of trouble and anxiety, turned his steps homeward.

As he approached the village he met a number of people, but none whom he knew, which somewhat surprised him, for he had thought himself acquainted with every one in the country round. Their dress, too, was of a different fashion from that to which he was accustomed. They all stared at him with equal marks of surprise, and whenever they cast their eyes upon him, invariably stroked their chins. The constant recurrence of this gesture induced Rip, involuntarily, to do the same, when to his astonishment, he found his beard had grown a foot long!

He had now entered the skirts of the village. A troop of strange children ran at his heels, hooting after him, and pointing at his gray beard. The dogs, too, not one of which he recognized for an old acquaintance, barked at him as he passed. The very village was altered; it was larger and more populous. There were rows of houses which he had never seen before, and those which had been his familiar haunts had disappeared. Strange names were over the doors - strange faces at the windows - every thing was strange. His mind now misgave him; he began to doubt whether both he and the world around him were not bewitched. Surely this was his native village, which he had left but the day before. There stood the Kaatskill mountains - there ran the silver Hudson at a distance - there was every hill and dale precisely as it had always been - Rip was sorely perplexed - "That flagon last night," thought he, "has addled my poor head sadly!"

It was with some difficulty that he found the way to his own house, which he approached with silent awe, expecting every moment to hear the shrill voice of Dame Van Winkle. He found the house gone to decay - the roof fallen in, the windows shattered, and the doors off the hinges. A half-starved dog that looked like Wolf was skulking about it. Rip called him by name, but the cur snarled, showed his teeth, and passed on. This was an unkind cut indeed - "My very dog," sighed poor Rip, "has forgotten me!"

He entered the house, which, to tell the truth, Dame Van Winkle had always kept in neat order. It was empty, forlorn, and apparently abandoned. This desolateness overcame all his connubial fears - he called loudly for his wife and children - the lonely chambers rang for a moment with his voice, and then all again was silence.

He now hurried forth, and hastened to his old resort, the village inn - but it too was gone. A large rickety wooden building stood in its place, with great gaping windows, some of them broken and mended with old hats and petticoats, and over the door was painted, "the Union Hotel, by Jonathan Doolittle." Instead of the great tree that used to shelter the quiet little Dutch inn of yore, there now was reared a tall naked pole, with something on the top that looked like a red night-cap, and from it was fluttering a flag, on which was a singular assemblage of stars and stripes - all this was strange and incomprehensible. He recognized on the sign, however, the ruby face of King George, under which he had smoked so many a peaceful pipe; but even this was singularly metamorphosed. The red coat was changed for one of blue and buff, a sword was held in the hand instead of a sceptre, the head was decorated with a cocked hat, and underneath was painted in large characters, GENERAL WASHINGTON.

There was, as usual, a crowd of folk about the door, but none that Rip recollected. The very character of the people seemed changed. There was a busy, bustling, disputatious tone about it, instead of the accustomed phlegm and drowsy tranquillity. He looked in vain for the sage Nicholas Vedder, with his broad face, double chin, and fair long pipe, uttering clouds of tobacco-smoke instead of idle speeches; or Van Bummel, the schoolmaster, doling forth the contents of an ancient newspaper. In place of these, a lean, bilious-looking fellow, with his pockets full of handbills, was haranguing vehemently about rights of citizens - elections - members of congress - liberty - Bunker's Hill - heroes of seventy-six - and other words, which were a perfect Babylonish jargon to the bewildered Van Winkle.

The appearance of Rip, with his long grizzled beard, his rusty fowling-piece, his uncouth dress, and an army of women and children at his heels, soon attracted the attention of the tavern politicians. They crowded round him, eyeing him from head to foot with great curiosity. The orator bustled up to him, and, drawing him partly aside, inquired "on which side he voted?" Rip stared in vacant stupidity. Another short but busy little fellow pulled him by the arm, and, rising on tiptoe, inquired in his ear, "Whether he was Federal or Democrat?" Rip was equally at a loss to comprehend the question; when a knowing, self-important old gentleman, in a sharp cocked hat, made his way through the crowd, putting them to the right and left with his elbows as he passed, and planting himself before Van Winkle, with one arm akimbo, the other resting on his cane, his keen eyes and sharp hat penetrating, as it were, into his very soul, demanded in an austere tone, "what brought him to the election with a gun on his shoulder, and a mob at his heels, and whether he meant to breed a riot in the village?" - "Alas! gentlemen," cried Rip, somewhat dismayed, "I am a poor quiet man, a native of the place, and a loyal subject of the king, God bless him!"

Here a general shout burst from the by-standers - "A tory! a tory! a spy! a refugee! hustle him! away with him!" It was with great difficulty that the self-important man in the cocked hat restored order; and, having assumed a tenfold austerity of brow, demanded again of the unknown culprit, what he came there for, and whom he was seeking? The poor man humbly assured him that he meant no harm, but merely came there in search of some of his neighbors, who used to keep about the tavern.

"Well - who are they? - name them."

Rip bethought himself a moment, and inquired, "Where's Nicholas Vedder?"

There was a silence for a little while, when an old man replied, in a thin piping voice, "Nicholas Vedder! why, he is dead and gone these eighteen years! There was a wooden tombstone in the church-yard that used to tell all about him, but that's rotten and gone too."

Rip

"W here's Brom Dutcher?"

"Oh, he went off to the army in the beginning of the war; some say he was killed at the storming of Stony Point - others say he was drowned in a squall at the foot of Antony's Nose. I don't know - he never came back again."

"Where's Van Bummel, the schoolmaster?"

"He went off to the wars too, was a great militia general, and is now in congress."

Rip's heart died away at hearing of these sad changes in his home and friends, and finding himself thus alone in the world. Every answer puzzled him too, by treating of such enormous lapses of time, and of matters which he could not understand: war - congress - Stony Point; - he had no courage to ask after any more friends, but cried out in despair, "Does nobody here know Rip Van Winkle?"

"Oh, Rip Van Winkle!" exclaimed two or three, "Oh, to be sure! that's Rip Van Winkle yonder, leaning against the tree."

Rip looked, and beheld a precise counterpart of himself, as he went up the mountain: apparently as lazy, and certainly as ragged. The poor fellow was now completely confounded. He doubted his own identity, and whether he was himself or another man. In the midst of his bewilderment, the man in the cocked hat demanded who he was, and what was his name?

"God knows," exclaimed he, at his wit's end; "I'm not myself - I'm somebody else - that's me yonder - no - that's somebody else got into my shoes - I was myself last night, but I fell asleep on the mountain, and they've changed my gun, and every thing's changed, and I'm changed, and I can't tell what's my name, or who I am!"

The by-standers began now to look at each other, nod, wink significantly, and tap their fingers against their foreheads. There was a whisper also, about securing the gun, and keeping the old fellow from doing mischief, at the very suggestion of which the self-important man in the cocked hat retired with some precipitation. At this critical moment a fresh comely woman pressed through the throng to get a peep at the gray-bearded man. She had a chubby child in her arms, which, frightened at his looks, began to cry. "Hush, Rip," cried she, "hush, you little fool; the old man won't hurt you." The name of the child, the air of the mother, the tone of her voice, all awakened a train of recollections in his mind. "What is your name, my good woman?" asked he.

"Judith Gardenier."

"And your father's name?"

"Ah, poor man, Rip Van Winkle was his name, but it's twenty years since he went away from home with his gun, and never has been heard of since - his dog came home without him; but whether he shot himself, or was carried away by the Indians, nobody can tell. I was then but a little girl."

Rip had but one question more to ask; but he put it with a faltering voice:

"Where's your mother?"

"Oh, she too had died but a short time since; she broke a blood-vessel in a fit of passion at a New-England peddler."

There was a drop of comfort, at least, in this intelligence. The honest man could contain himself no longer. He caught his daughter and her child in his arms. "I am your father!" cried he - "Young Rip Van Winkle once - old Rip Van Winkle now! - Does nobody know poor Rip Van Winkle?"

All stood amazed, until an old woman, tottering out from among the crowd, put her hand to her brow, and peering under it in his face for a moment, exclaimed, "Sure enough! it is Rip Van Winkle - it is himself! Welcome home again, old neighbor - Why, where have you been these twenty long years?"

Rip's story was soon told, for the whole twenty years had been to him but as one night. The neighbors stared when they heard it; some were seen to wink at each other, and put their tongues in their cheeks: and the self-important man in the cocked hat, who, when the alarm was over, had returned to the field, screwed down the corners of his mouth, and shook his head - upon which there was a general shaking of the head throughout the assemblage.

The old Rip Van Winkle house burned to the ground in 1918.

It was determined, however, to take the opinion of old Peter Van-
derdonk, who was seen slowly advancing up the road. He was
a descendant of the historian of that name, who wrote one of
the earliest accounts of the province. Peter was the most ancient
inhabitant of the village, and well versed in all the wonderful events
and traditions of the neighborhood. He recollected Rip at once, and
corroborated his story in the most satisfactory manner. He assured the
company that it was a fact, handed down from his ancestor the historian, that the Kaatskill mountains had always been haunted by strange
beings. That it was affirmed that the great Hendrick Hudson, the first
discoverer of the river and country, kept a kind of vigil there every twenty years, with his crew of the Half-moon; being permitted in this way
to revisit the scenes of his enterprise, and keep a guardian eye upon the
river, and the great city called by his name. That his father had once seen
them in their old Dutch dresses playing at nine-pins in a hollow of the
mountain; and that he himself had heard, one summer afternoon, the
sound of their balls, like distant peals of thunder.

To make a long story short, the company broke up, and returned to the more important concerns of the election. Rip's daughter
took him home to live with her; she had a snug, well-furnished house,
and a stout cheery farmer for a husband, whom Rip recollected for one
of the urchins that used to climb upon his back. As to Rip's son and
heir, who was the ditto of himself, seen leaning against the tree, he was
employed to work on the farm; but evinced an hereditary disposition to
attend to anything else but his business.

Rip now resumed his old walks and habits; he soon found many
of his former cronies, though all rather the worse for the wear and tear
of time; and preferred making friends among the rising generation, with
whom he soon grew into great favor.

Having nothing to do at home, and being arrived at that happy
age when a man can be idle with impunity, he took his place once more
on the bench at the inn door, and was reverenced as one of the patri-
archs of the village, and a chronicle of the old times "before the war."

It was some time before he could get into the regular track of gossip, or could be made to comprehend the strange events that had taken place during his torpor. How that there had been a revolutionary war - that the country had thrown off the yoke of old England - and that, instead of being a subject of his Majesty George the Third, he was now a free citizen of the United States. Rip, in fact, was no politician; the changes of states and empires made but little impression on him; but there was one species of despotism under which he had long groaned, and that was - petticoat government. Happily that was at an end; he had got his neck out of the yoke of matrimony, and could go in and out whenever he pleased, without dreading the tyranny of Dame Van Winkle. Whenever her name was mentioned, however, he shook his head, shrugged his shoulders, and cast up his eyes; which might pass either for an expression of resignation to his fate, or joy at his deliverance.

He used to tell his story to every stranger that arrived at Mr. Doolittle's hotel. He was observed, at first, to vary on some points every time he told it, which was, doubtless, owing to his having so recently awaked. It at last settled down precisely to the tale I have related, and not a man, woman, or child in the neighborhood, but knew it by heart. Some always pretended to doubt the reality of it, and insisted that Rip had been out of his head, and that this was one point on which he always remained flighty. The old Dutch inhabitants, however, almost universally gave it full credit. Even to this day they never hear a thunderstorm of a summer afternoon about the Kaatskill, but they say Hendrick Hudson and his crew are at their game of nine-pins; and it is a common wish of all hen-pecked husbands in the neighborhood, when life hangs heavy on their hands, that they might have a quieting draught out of Rip Van Winkle's flagon.

Mountjoy

Or Some Passages Out Of The Life Of A Castle-Builder

I was born among romantic scenery, in one of the wildest parts of the Hudson, which at that time was not so thickly settled as at present. My father was descended from one of the old Huguenot families that came over to this country on the revocation of the edict of Nantz. He lived in a style of easy, rural independence, on a patrimonial estate that had been for two or three generations in the family. He was an indolent, good-natured man, who took the world as it went, and had a kind of laughing philosophy, that parried all rubs and mishaps, and served him in the place of wisdom. This was the part of his character least to my taste; for I was of an enthusiastic, excitable temperament, prone to kindle up with new schemes and projects, and he was apt to dash my sallying enthusiasm by some unlucky joke; so that whenever I was in a glow with any sudden excitement, I stood in mortal dread of his good-humor.

Yet he indulged me in every vagary; for I was an only son, and of course a personage of importance in the household. I had two sisters older than myself, and one younger. The former were educated at New York, under the eye of a maiden aunt; the latter remained at home, and was my cherished playmate, the companion of my thoughts. We were two imaginative little beings, of quick susceptibility, and prone to see wonders and mysteries in everything around us. Scarce had we learned to read, when our mother made us holiday presents of all the nursery literature of the day; which at that time consisted of little books covered with gilt paper, adorned with "cuts," and filled with tales of fairies, giants, and enchanters. What draughts of delightful fiction did we then inhale! My sister Sophy was of a soft and tender nature. She would weep over the woes of the *Children in the Wood*, or quake at the dark romance of *Blue-Beard*, and the terrible mysteries of the blue chamber. But I was all for enterprise and adventure. I burned to emulate the deeds of that heroic prince who delivered the white cat from her enchantment; or he of no less royal blood, and doughty enterprise, who broke the charmed slumber of the *Beauty in the Wood*!

The house in which we lived was just the kind of place to foster such propensities. It was a venerable mansion, half villa, half farmhouse. The oldest part was of stone, with loop-holes for musketry, having served as a family fortress in the time of the Indians. To this there had been made various additions, some of brick, some of wood, according to the exigencies of the moment; so that it was full of nooks and crooks, and chambers of all sorts and sizes. It was buried among willows, elms, and cherry trees, and surrounded with roses and hollyhocks, with honeysuckle and sweetbrier clambering about every window. A brood of hereditary pigeons sunned themselves upon the roof; hereditary swallows and martins built about the eaves and chimneys; and hereditary bees hummed about the flower-beds.

Under the influence of our story-books every object around us now assumed a new character, and a charmed interest. The wild flowers were no longer the mere ornaments of the fields, or the resorts of the toil-

A view of the Hudson River.

ful bee; they were the lurking-places of fairies. We would watch the humming-bird, as it hovered around the trumpet creeper at our porch, and the butterfly as it flitted up into the blue air, above the sunny tree-tops, and fancy them some of the tiny beings from fairyland. I would call to mind all that I had read of Robin Goodfellow and his power of transformation. Oh, how I envied him that power! How I longed to be able to compress my form into utter littleness; to ride the bold dragonfly; swing on the tall bearded grass; follow the ant into his subterraneous habitation, or dive into the cavernous depths of the honeysuckle!

While I was yet a mere child I was sent to a daily school, about two miles distant. The schoolhouse was on the edge of a wood, close by a brook overhung with birches, alders, and dwarf willows. We of the school who lived at some distance came with our dinners put up in little baskets. In the intervals of school hours we would gather round a spring, under a tuft of hazel-bushes, and have a kind of picnic; interchanging the rustic dainties with which our provident mothers had fitted us out. Then, when our joyous repast was over, and my companions were disposed for play, I would draw forth one of my cherished story-books, stretch myself on the green sward, and soon lose myself in its bewitching contents.

I became an oracle among my schoolmates on account of my superior erudition, and soon imparted to them the contagion of my infected fancy. Often in the evening, after school hours, we would sit on the trunk of some fallen tree in the woods, and vie with each other in telling extravagant stories, until the whip-poor-will began his nightly moaning, and the fireflies sparkled in the gloom. Then came the perilous journey homeward. What delight we would take in getting up wanton panics in some dusky part of the wood; scampering like frightened deer; pausing to take breath; renewing the panic, and scampering off again, wild with fictitious terror!

Our greatest trial was to pass a dark, lonely pool, covered with pond-lilies, peopled with bullfrogs and water snakes, and haunted by two white cranes. Oh! the terrors of that pond! How our little hearts would beat as we approached it; what fearful glances we would throw around!

And if by chance a plash of a wild duck, or the guttural twang of a bull-frog, struck our ears, as we stole quietly by--away we sped, nor paused until completely out of the woods. Then, when I reached home, what a world of adventures and imaginary terrors would I have to relate to my sister Sophy!

As I advanced in years, this turn of mind increased upon me, and became more confirmed. I abandoned myself to the impulses of a romantic imagination, which controlled my studies, and gave a bias to all my habits. My father observed me continually with a book in my hand, and satisfied himself that I was a profound student; but what were my studies? Works of fiction; tales of chivalry; voyages of discovery; travels in the East; everything, in short, that partook of adventure and romance. I well remember with what zest I entered upon that part of my studies which treated of the heathen mythology, and particularly of the sylvan deities. Then indeed my school books became dear to me. The neighborhood was well calculated to foster the reveries of a mind like mine. It abounded with solitary retreats, wild streams, solemn forests, and silent valleys. I would ramble about for a whole day with a volume of Ovid's *Metamorphoses* in my pocket, and work myself into a kind of self-delusion, so as to identify the surrounding scenes with those of which I had just been reading. I would loiter about a brook that glided through the shadowy depths of the forest, picturing it to myself the haunt of Naiads. I would steal round some bushy copse that opened upon a glade, as if I expected to come suddenly upon Diana and her nymphs, or to behold Pan and his satyrs bounding, with whoop and halloo, through the woodland. I would throw myself, during the panting heats of a summer noon, under the shade of some wide-spreading tree, and muse and dream away the hours, in a state of mental intoxication. I drank in the very light of day, as nectar, and my soul seemed to bathe with ecstasy in the deep blue of a summer sky.

In these wanderings nothing occurred to jar my feelings, or bring me back to the realities of life. There is a repose in our mighty forests that gives full scope to the imagination. Now and then I would hear the distant sound of the woodcutter's ax, or the crash of some tree which he had laid low; but these noises, echoing along the quiet landscape, could easily be wrought by fancy into harmony with its illusions. In general, however, the woody recesses of the neighborhood were peculiarly wild and unfrequented. I could ramble for a whole day, without coming upon any traces of cultivation. The partridge of the wood scarcely seemed to shun my path, and the squirrel, from his nut-tree, would gaze at me for an instant, with sparkling eye, as if wondering at the unwonted intrusion.

I cannot help dwelling on this delicious period of my life; when as yet I had known no sorrow, nor experienced any worldly care. I have since studied much, both of books and men, and of course have grown too wise to be so easily pleased; yet with all my wisdom, I must confess I look back with a secret feeling of regret to the days of happy ignorance before I had begun to be a philosopher.

It must be evident that I was in a hopeful training for one who was to descend into the arena of life, and wrestle with the world. The tutor, also, who superintended my studies in the more advanced stage of my education, was just fitted to complete the fata morgana which was forming in my mind. His name was Glencoe. He was a pale, melancholy-looking man, about forty years of age; a native of Scotland, liberally educated, and who had devoted himself to the instruction of youth from taste rather than necessity; for, as he said, he loved the human heart, and delighted to study it in its earlier impulses. My two elder sisters, having returned home from a city boarding-school, were likewise placed under his care, to direct their reading in history and belles-lettres.

We all soon became attached to Glencoe. It is true, we were at first somewhat prepossessed against him. His meager, pallid countenance, his broad pronunciation, his inattention to the little forms of society, and an awkward and embarrassed manner, on first acquaintance, were much against him; but we soon discovered that under this unpromising exterior existed the kindest urbanity of temper; the warmest sympathies; the most enthusiastic benevolence. His mind was ingenious and acute. His reading had been various, but more abstruse than profound; his memory was stored, on all subjects, with facts, theories, and quotations, and crowded with crude materials for thinking. These, in a moment of excitement, would be, as it were, melted down, and poured forth in the lava of a heated imagination. At such moments, the change in the whole man was wonderful. His meager form would acquire a dignity and grace; his long, pale visage would flash with a hectic glow; his eyes would beam with intense speculation; and there would be pathetic tones and deep modulations in his voice, that delighted the ear, and spoke movingly to the heart.

But what most endeared him to us was the kindness and sympathy with which he entered into all our interests and wishes. Instead of curbing and checking our young imaginations with the reins of sober reason, he was a little too apt to catch the impulse and be hurried away with us. He could not withstand the excitement of any sally of feeling or fancy, and was prone to lend heightening tints to the illusive coloring of youthful anticipation.

Under his guidance my sisters and myself soon entered upon a more extended range of studies; but while they wandered, with delighted minds, through the wide field of history and belles-lettres, a nobler walk was opened to my superior intellect.

The mind of Glencoe presented a singular mixture of philosophy and poetry. He was fond of metaphysics and prone to indulge in abstract speculations, though his metaphysics were somewhat fine spun and fanciful, and his speculations were apt to partake of what my father most irreverently termed "humbug." For my part, I delighted in them, and the more especially because they set my father to sleep and completely confounded my sisters. I entered with my accustomed eagerness into this new branch of study. Metaphysics were now my passion. My sisters attempted to accompany me, but they soon faltered, and gave out before they had got half way through Smith's *Theory of the Moral Sentiments*. I, however, went on, exulting in my strength. Glencoe supplied me with books, and I devoured them with appetite, if not digestion. We walked and talked together under the trees before the house, or sat apart, like Milton's angels, and held high converse upon themes beyond the grasp of ordinary intellects. Glencoe possessed a kind of philosophic chivalry, in imitation of the old peripatetic sages, and was continually dreaming of romantic enterprises in morals, and splendid systems for the improvement of society. He had a fanciful mode of illustrating abstract subjects, peculiarly to my taste; clothing them with the language of poetry, and throwing round them almost the magic hues of fiction. "How charming," thought I, "is divine philosophy;" not harsh and crabbed, as dull fools suppose,"But a perpetual feast of nectar'd sweets, Where no crude surfeit reigns."

I felt a wonderful self-complacency at being on such excellent terms with a man whom I considered on a parallel with the sages of antiquity, and looked down with a sentiment of pity on the feebler intellects of my sisters, who could comprehend nothing of metaphysics. It is true, when I attempted to study them by myself, I was apt to get in a fog; but when Glencoe came to my aid, everything was soon as clear to me as day. My ear drank in the beauty of his words; my imagination was dazzled with the splendor of his illustrations. It caught up the sparkling sands of poetry that glittered through his speculations, and mistook them for the golden ore of wisdom. Struck with the facility with which I seemed to imbibe and relish the most abstract doctrines, I conceived a still higher opinion of my mental powers, and was convinced that I also was a philosopher.

I was now verging toward man's estate, and though my education had been extremely irregular--following the caprices of my humor, which I mistook for the impulses of my genius--yet I was regarded with wonder and delight by my mother and sisters, who considered me almost as wise and infallible as I considered myself. This high opinion of me was strengthened by a declamatory habit, which made me an oracle and orator at the domestic board. The time was now at hand, however, that was to put my philosophy to the test.

We had passed through a long winter, and the spring at length opened upon us with unusual sweetness. The soft serenity of the weather;

the beauty of the surrounding country; the joyous notes of the birds; the balmy breath of flower and blossom, all combined to fill my bosom with indistinct sensations, and nameless wishes. Amid the soft seductions of the season, I lapsed into a state of utter indolence, both of body and mind.

Philosophy had lost its charms for me. Metaphysics -- faugh! I tried to study; took down volume after volume, ran my eye vacantly over a few pages, and threw them by with distaste. I loitered about the house, with my hands in my pockets, and an air of complete vacancy. Something was necessary to make me happy; but what was that something? I sauntered to the apartments of my sisters, hoping their conversation might amuse me. They had walked out, and the room was vacant. On the table lay a volume which they had been reading. It was a novel. I had never read a novel, having conceived a contempt for works of the kind, from hearing them universally condemned. It is true, I had remarked that they were as universally read; but I considered them beneath the attention of a philosopher, and never would venture to read them, lest I should lessen my mental superiority in the eyes of my sisters. Nay, I had taken up a work of the kind now and then, when I knew my sisters were observing me, looked into it for a moment, and then laid it down, with a slight supercilious smile. On the present occasion, out of mere listlessness, I took up the volume and turned over a few of the first pages. I thought I heard some one coming, and laid it down. I was mistaken; no one was near, and what I had read tempted my curiosity to read a little further. I leaned against a window-frame, and in a few minutes was completely lost in the story. How long I stood there reading I know not, but I believe for nearly two hours. Suddenly I heard my sisters on the stairs, when I thrust the book into my bosom, and the two other volumes which lay near into my pockets, and hurried out of the house to my beloved woods. Here I remained all day beneath the trees, bewildered, bewitched, devouring the contents of these delicious volumes, and only returned to the house when it was too dark to peruse their pages.

This novel finished, I replaced it in my sisters' apartment, and looked for others. Their stock was ample, for they had brought home all that were current in the city; but my appetite demanded an immense supply. All this course of reading was carried on clandestinely, for I was a little ashamed of it, and fearful that my wisdom might be called in question; but this very privacy gave it additional zest. It was "bread eaten in secret"; it had the charm of a private amour.

But think what must have been the effect of such a course of reading on a youth of my temperament and turn of mind; indulged, too, amid romantic scenery and in the romantic season of the year. It seemed as if I had entered upon a new scene of existence. A train of combustible feelings were lighted up in me, and my soul was all tenderness and passion. Never was youth more completely love-sick, though as yet it was a mere general sentiment, and wanted a definite object. Unfortunately, our neighborhood was particularly deficient in female society, and I languished in vain for some divinity to whom I might offer up this most uneasy burden of affections. I was at one time seriously enamored of a lady whom I saw occasionally in my rides, reading at the window of a country-seat; and actually serenaded her with my flute; when, to my confusion, I discovered that she was old enough to be my mother. It was a sad damper to my romance; especially as my father heard of it, and made it the subject of one of those household jokes which he was apt to serve up at every meal-time.

I soon recovered from this check, however, but it was only to relapse into a state of amorous excitement. I passed whole days in the fields, and along the brooks; for there is something in the tender passion that makes us alive to the beauties of nature. A soft sunshiny morning infused a sort of rapture into my breast. I flung open my arms, like the Grecian youth in Ovid, as if I would take in and embrace the balmy atmosphere. The song of the birds melted me to tenderness. I would lie by the side of some rivulet for hours, and form garlands of the flowers on its banks, and muse on ideal beauties, and sigh from the crowd of undefined emotions that swelled my bosom.

In this state of amorous delirium, I was strolling one morning along a beautiful wild brook, which I had discovered in a glen. There was one place where a small waterfall, leaping from among rocks into a natural basin, made a scene such as a poet might have chosen as the haunt of some shy Naiad. It was here I usually retired to banquet on my novels. In visiting the place this morning I traced distinctly, on the margin of the basin, which was of fine clear sand, the prints of a female foot of the most slender and delicate proportions. This was sufficient for an imagination like mine. Robinson Crusoe himself, when he discovered the print of a savage foot on the beach of his lonely island, could not have been more suddenly assailed with thick-coming fancies.

I endeavored to track the steps, but they only passed for a few paces along the fine sand, and then were lost among the herbage. I remained gazing in reverie upon this passing trace of loveliness. It evidently was not made by any of my sisters, for they knew nothing of this haunt; besides, the foot was smaller than theirs; it was remarkable for its beautiful delicacy.

My eye accidentally caught two or three half-withered wild flowers lying on the ground. The unknown nymph had doubtless dropped them from her bosom! Here was a new document of taste and sentiment. I treasured them up as invaluable relics. The place, too, where I found them, was remarkably picturesque, and the most beautiful part of the brook. It was overhung with a fine elm, entwined with grapevines. She who could select such a spot, who could delight in wild brooks, and wild flowers, and silent solitudes, must have fancy, and feeling, and tenderness; and with all these qualities, she must be beautiful!

But who could be this Unknown, that had thus passed by, as in a morning dream, leaving merely flowers and fairy footsteps to tell of her loveliness? There was a mystery in it that bewildered me. It was so vague and disembodied, like those "airy tongues that syllable men's names" in solitude. Every attempt to solve the mystery was vain. I could hear of no being in the neighborhood to whom this trace could be ascribed. I haunted the spot, and became daily more and more enamored. Never, surely, was passion more pure and spiritual, and never lover in more dubious situation. My case could be compared only to that of the amorous prince in the fairy tale of Cinderella; but he had a glass slipper on which to lavish his tenderness. I, alas! was in love with a footstep!

The imagination is alternately a cheat and a dupe; nay, more, it is the most subtle of cheats, for it cheats itself and becomes the dupe of its own delusions. It conjures up "airy nothings," gives to them a "local habitation and a name," and then bows to their control as implicitly as though they were realities. Such was now my case. The good Numa could not more thoroughly have persuaded himself that the nymph Egeria hovered about her sacred fountain and communed with him in spirit than I had deceived myself into a kind of visionary intercourse with the airy phantom fabricated in my brain. I constructed a rustic seat at the foot of the tree where I had discovered the footsteps. I made a kind of bower there, where I used to pass my mornings reading poetry and romances. I carved hearts and darts on the tree, and hung it with garlands. My heart was full to overflowing, and wanted some faithful bosom into which it might relieve itself. What is a lover without a confidante? I thought at once of my sister Sophy, my early playmate, the sister of my affections. She was so reasonable, too, and of such correct feelings, always listening to my words as oracular sayings, and admiring my scraps of poetry as the very inspirations of the muse. From such a devoted, such a rational being, what secrets could I have?

I accordingly took her one morning to my favorite retreat. She looked around, with delighted surprise, upon the rustic seat, the bower, the tree carved with emblems of the tender passion. She turned her eyes upon me to inquire the meaning.

"Oh, Sophy," exclaimed I, clasping both her hands in mine, and looking earnestly in her face, "I am in love."

She started with surprise.

"Sit down," said I, "and I will tell you all."

She seated herself upon the rustic bench, and I went into a full history of the footstep, with all the associations of idea that had been conjured up by my imagination.

Sophy was enchanted; it was like a fairy tale; she had read of such mysterious visitations in books, and the loves thus conceived were always for beings of superior order, and were always happy. She caught the illusion in all its force; her cheek glowed; her eye brightened.

"I daresay she's pretty," said Sophy.

"Pretty!" echoed I, "she is beautiful." I went through all the reasoning by which I had logically proved the fact to my own satisfaction. I dwelt upon the evidences of her taste, her sensibility to the beauties of nature; her soft meditative habit that delighted in solitude. "Oh," said I, clasping my hands, "to have such a companion to wander through these scenes; to sit with her by this murmuring stream; to wreathe garlands round her brows; to hear the music of her voice mingling with the whisperings of these groves; to --"

"Delightful! delightful!" cried Sophy; "what a sweet creature she must be! She is just the friend I want. How I shall dote upon her! Oh, my dear brother! you must not keep her all to yourself. You must let me have some share of her!"

I caught her to my bosom: "You shall -- you shall!" cried I, "my dear Sophy; we will all live for each other!"

The conversation with Sophy heightened the illusions of my mind; and the manner in which she had treated my daydream identified it with facts and persons and gave it still more the stamp of reality. I walked about as one in a trance, heedless of the world around and lapped in an elysium of the fancy.

In this mood I met one morning with Glencoe. He accosted me with his usual smile, and was proceeding with some general observations, but paused and fixed on me an inquiring eye.

"What is the matter with you?" said he, "you seem agitated; has anything in particular happened?"

"Nothing," said I, hesitating; "at least nothing worth communicating to you."

"Nay, my dear young friend," said he, "whatever is of sufficient importance to agitate you is worthy of being communicated to me."

"Well; but my thoughts are running on what you would think a frivolous subject."

"No subject is frivolous that has the power to awaken strong feelings."

"What think you," said I, hesitating, "what think you of love?"

Glencoe almost started at the question. "Do you call that a frivolous subject?" replied he. "Believe me, there is none fraught with such deep, such vital interest. If you talk, indeed, of the capricious inclination awakened by the mere charm of perishable beauty, I grant it to be idle in the extreme; but that love which springs from the concordant sympathies of virtuous hearts; that love which is awakened by the perception of moral excellence, and fed by meditation on intellectual as well as personal beauty; that is a passion which refines and ennobles the human heart. Oh, where is there a sight more nearly approaching to the intercourse of angels, than that of two young beings, free from the sins and follies of the world, mingling pure thoughts, and looks, and feelings, and becoming, as it were, soul of one soul and heart of one heart! How exquisite the silent converse that they hold; the soft devotion of the eye, that needs no words to make it eloquent! Yes, my friend, if there be anything in this weary world worthy of heaven, it is the pure bliss of such a mutual affection!"

The words of my worthy tutor overcame all further reserve. "Mr. Glencoe," cried I, blushing still deeper, "I am in love."

"And is that what you were ashamed to tell me? Oh, never seek to conceal from your friend so important a secret. If your passion be unworthy, it is for the steady hand of friendship to pluck it forth; if honorable, none but an enemy would seek to stifle it. On nothing does the character and happiness so much depend as on the first affection of the heart. Were you caught by some fleeting and superficial charm--a bright eye, a blooming cheek, a soft voice, or a voluptuous form--I would warn you to beware; I would tell you that beauty is but a passing gleam of the morning, a perishable flower; that accident may becloud and blight it, and that at best it must soon pass away. But were you in love with such a one as I could describe; young in years, but still younger in feelings; lovely in person, but as a type of the mind's beauty; soft in voice, in token of gentleness of spirit; blooming in countenance, like the rosy tints of morning kindling with the promise of a genial day; an eye beaming with the benignity of a happy heart; a cheerful temper, alive to all kind impulses, and frankly diffusing its own felicity; a self-poised mind, that needs not lean on others for support; an elegant taste, that can embellish solitude, and furnish out its own enjoyments--"

"My dear sir," cried I, for I could contain myself no longer, "you have described the very person!"

"Why, then, my dear young friend," said he, affectionately pressing my hand, "in God's name, love on!"

For the remainder of the day I was in some such state of dreamy beatitude as a Turk is said to enjoy when under the influence of opium. It must be already manifest how prone I was to bewilder myself with picturings of the fancy, so as to confound them with existing realities. In the present instance, Sophy and Glencoe had contributed to promote the transient delusion. Sophy, dear girl, had as usual joined with me in my castle-building, and indulged in the same train of imaginings, while Glencoe, duped by my enthusiasm, firmly believed that I spoke of a being I had seen and known. By their sympathy with my feelings they in a manner became associated with the Unknown in my mind, and thus linked her with the circle of my intimacy.

In the evening, our family party was assembled in the hall, to enjoy the refreshing breeze. Sophy was playing some favorite Scotch airs on the piano, while Glencoe, seated apart, with his forehead resting on his hand, was buried in one of those pensive reveries that made him so interesting to me.

"What a fortunate being I am!" thought I, "blessed with such a sister and such a friend! I have only to find out this amiable Unknown, to wed her, and be happy! What a paradise will be my home, graced with a partner of such exquisite refinement! It will be a perfect fairy bower, buried among sweets and roses. Sophy shall live with us, and be the companion of all our enjoyments. Glencoe, too, shall no more be the solitary being that he now appears. He shall have a home with us. He shall have his study, where, when he pleases, he may shut himself up from the world, and bury himself in his own reflections. His retreat shall be sacred; no one shall intrude there; no one but myself, who will visit him now and then, in his seclusion, where we will devise grand schemes together for the improvement of mankind. How delightfully our days will pass, in a round of rational pleasures and elegant employments! Sometimes we will have music; sometimes we will read; sometimes we will wander through the flower garden, when I will smile with complacency on every flower my wife has planted; while in the long winter evenings the ladies will sit at their work, and listen with hushed attention to Glencoe and myself, as we discuss the abstruse doctrines of metaphysics."

From this delectable reverie, I was startled by my father's slapping me on the shoulder. "What possesses the lad?" cried he; "here have I been speaking to you half a dozen times, without receiving an answer."

"Pardon me, sir," replied I; "I was so completely lost in thought, that I did not hear you."

"Lost in thought! And pray what were you thinking of? Some of your philosophy, I suppose."

"Upon my word," said my sister Charlotte, with an arch laugh, "I suspect Harry's in love again."

"And if were in love, Charlotte," said I, somewhat nettled, and recollecting Glencoe's enthusiastic eulogy of the passion, "if I were in love, is that a matter of jest and laughter? Is the tenderest and most fervid affection that can animate the human breast to be made a matter of cold-hearted ridicule?"

My sister colored. "Certainly not, brother! -- nor did I mean to make it so, or to say anything that should wound your feelings. Had I really suspected you had formed some genuine attachment, it would have been sacred in my eyes; but -- but," said she, smiling, as if at some whimsical recollection, "I thought that you -- you might be indulging in another little freak of the imagination."

"I'll wager any money," cried my father, "he has fallen in love again with some old lady at a window!"

"Oh, no!" cried my dear sister Sophy, with the most gracious warmth; "she is young and beautiful."

"From what I understand," said Glencoe, rousing himself, "she must be lovely in mind as in person."

I found my friends were getting me into a fine scrape. I began to perspire at every pore, and felt my ears tingle.

"Well, but," cried my father, "who is she? -- what is she? Let us hear something about her."

This was no time to explain so delicate a matter. I caught up my hat, and vanished out of the house.

The moment I was in the open air, and alone, my heart upbraided me. Was this respectful treatment to my father--to such a father, too--who had always regarded me as the pride of his age--the staff of his hopes? It is true, he was apt sometimes to laugh at my enthusiastic flights, and did not treat my philosophy with due respect; but when had he ever thwarted a wish of my heart? Was I then to act with reserve toward him, in a matter which might affect the whole current of my future life? "I have done wrong," thought I; "but it is not too late to remedy it.
I will hasten back and open my whole heart to my father!"

I returned accordingly, and was just on the point of entering the house, with my heart full of filial piety and a contrite speech upon my lips, when I heard a burst of obstreperous laughter from my father, and a loud titter from my two elder sisters.

"A footstep!" shouted he, as soon as he could recover himself; "in love with a footstep! Why, this beats the old lady at the window!" And then there was another appalling burst of laughter. Had it been a clap of thunder, it could hardly have astounded me more completely. Sophy, in the simplicity of her heart, had told all, and had set my father's risible propensities in full action.

Never was poor mortal so thoroughly crestfallen as myself. The whole delusion was at an end. I drew off silently from the house, shrinking smaller and smaller at every fresh peal of laughter; and, wandering about until the family had retired, stole quietly to my bed. Scarce any sleep, however, visited my eyes that night! I lay overwhelmed with mortification, and meditating how I might meet the family in the morning. The idea of ridicule was always intolerable to me; but to endure it on a subject by which my feelings had been so much excited seemed worse than death. I almost determined, at one time, to get up, saddle my horse, and ride off, I knew not whither.

At length I came to a resolution. Before going down to breakfast, I sent for Sophy, and employed her as embassador to treat formally in the matter. I insisted that the subject should be buried in oblivion; otherwise I would not show my face at table. It was readily agreed to; for not one of the family would have given me pain for the world. They faithfully kept their promise. Not a word was said of the matter; but there were wry faces, and suppressed titters, that went to my soul; and whenever my father looked me in the face, it was with such a tragi-comical leer--such an attempt to pull down a serious brow upon a whimsical mouth--that I had a thousand times rather he had laughed outright.

For a day or two after the mortifying occurrence just related, I kept as much as possible out of the way of the family, and wandered about the fields and woods by myself. I was sadly out of tune; my feelings were all jarred and unstrung. The birds sang from every grove, but I took no pleasure in their melody; and the flowers of the field bloomed unheeded around me. To be crossed in love is bad enough; but then one can fly to poetry for relief, and turn one's woes to account in soul-subduing stanzas. But to have one's whole passion, object and all, annihilated, dispelled, proved to be such stuff as dreams are made of -- or, worse than all, to be turned into a proverb and a jest -- what consolation is there in such a case?

I avoided the fatal brook where I had seen the footstep. My favorite resort was now the banks of the Hudson, where I sat upon the rocks and mused upon the current that dimpled by, or the waves that laved the shore; or watched the bright mutations of the clouds, and the shifting lights and shadows of the distant mountain. By degrees a returning serenity stole over my feelings; and a sigh now and then, gentle and easy, and unattended by pain, showed that my heart was recovering its susceptibility.

As I was sitting in this musing mood my eye became gradually fixed upon an object that was borne along by the tide. It proved to be a little pinnace, beautifully modeled, and gayly painted and decorated. It was an unusual sight in this neighborhood, which was rather lonely; indeed, it was rare to see any pleasure-barks in this part of the river. As it drew nearer, I perceived that there was no one on board; it had apparently drifted from its anchorage. There was not a breath of air; the little bark came floating along on the glassy stream, wheeling about with the eddies. At length it ran aground, almost at the foot of the rock on which I was seated. I descended to the margin of the river, and drawing the bark to shore, admired its light and elegant proportions and the taste with which it was fitted up. The benches were covered with cushions, and its long streamer was of silk. On one of the cushion's lay a lady's glove, of delicate size and shape, with beautifully tapered fingers. I instantly seized it and thrust it in my bosom; it seemed a match for the fairy footstep that had so fascinated me.

In a moment all the romance of my bosom was again in a glow. Here was one of the very incidents of fairy tale; a bark sent by some invisible power, some good genius, or benevolent fairy, to waft me to some delectable adventure. I recollected something of an enchanted bark, drawn by white swans, that conveyed a knight down the current of the Rhine, on some enterprise connected with love and beauty. The glove, too, showed that there was a lady fair concerned in the present adventure. It might be a gauntlet of defiance, to dare me to the enterprise.

In the spirit of romance and the whim of the moment, I sprang on board, hoisted the light sail, and pushed from shore. As if breathed by some presiding power, a light breeze at that moment sprang up, swelled out the sail, and dallied with the silken streamer. For a time I glided along under steep umbrageous banks, or across deep sequestered bays; and then stood out over a wide expansion of the river toward a high rocky promontory. It was a lovely evening; the sun was setting in a congregation of clouds that threw the whole heavens in a glow, and were reflected in the river. I delighted myself with all kinds of fantastic fancies, as to what enchanted island, or mystic bower, or necromantic palace, I was to be conveyed by the fairy bark.

In the revel of my fancy I had not noticed that the gorgeous congregation of clouds which had so much delighted me was in fact a gathering thunder gust. I perceived the truth too late. The clouds came hurrying on, darkening as they advanced. The whole face of nature was suddenly changed, and assumed that baleful and livid tint, predictive of a storm. I tried to gain the shore, but before I could reach it a blast of wind struck the water and lashed it at once into foam. The next moment it overtook the boat. Alas! I was nothing of a sailor; and my protecting fairy forsook me in the moment of peril. I endeavored to lower the sail; but in so doing I had to quit the helm; the bark was overturned in an instant, and I was thrown into the water. I endeavored to cling to the wreck, but missed my hold; being a poor swimmer I soon found myself sinking, but grasped a light oar that was floating by me. It was not sufficient for my support; I again sank beneath the surface; there was a rushing and bubbling sound in my ears, and all sense forsook me.

How long I remained insensible, I know not. I had a confused notion of being moved and tossed about, and of hearing strange beings and strange voices around me; but all this was like a hideous dream. When I at length recovered full consciousness and perception, I found myself in bed in a spacious chamber, furnished with more taste than I had been accustomed to. The bright rays of a morning sun were intercepted by curtains of a delicate rose color, that gave a soft, voluptuous tinge to every object. Not far from my bed, on a classic tripod, was a basket of beautiful exotic flowers, breathing the sweetest fragrance.

"Where am I? How came I here?"

I tasked my mind to catch at some previous event, from which I might trace up the thread of existence to the present moment. By degrees I called to mind the fairy pinnace, my daring embarkation, my adventurous voyage, and my disastrous shipwreck. Beyond that, all was chaos. How came I here? What unknown region had I landed upon? The people that inhabited it must be gentle and amiable, and of elegant tastes, for they loved downy beds, fragrant flowers, and rose-colored curtains.

While I lay thus musing, the tones of a harp reached my ear. Presently they were accompanied by a female voice. It came from the room below; but in the profound stillness of my chamber not a modulation was lost. My sisters were all considered good musicians, and sang very tolerably; but I had never heard a voice like this. There was no attempt at difficult execution, or striking effect; but there were exquisite inflections, and tender turns, which art could not reach. Nothing but feeling and sentiment could produce them. It was soul breathed forth in sound. I was always alive to the influence of music; indeed, I was susceptible of voluptuous influences of every kind--sounds, colors, shapes, and fragrant odors. I was the very slave of sensation.

I lay mute and breathless, and drank in every note of this siren strain. It thrilled through my whole frame, and filled my soul with melody and love. I pictured to myself, with curious logic, the form of the unseen musician. Such melodious sounds and exquisite inflections could only be produced by organs of the most delicate flexibility. Such organs do not belong to coarse, vulgar forms; they are the harmonious results of fair proportions, and admirable symmetry. A being so organized must be lovely.

Again my busy imagination was at work. I called to mind the Arabian story of a prince, borne away during sleep by a good genius, to the distant abode of a princess of ravishing beauty. I do not pretend to say that I believed in having experienced a similar transportation; but it was my inveterate habit to cheat myself with fancies of the kind, and to give the tinge of illusion to surrounding realities.

The witching sound had ceased, but its vibrations still played round my heart, and filled it with a tumult of soft emotions. At this moment, a self-upbraiding pang shot through my bosom. "Ah, recreant!" a voice seemed to exclaim, "is this the stability of thine affections? What! hast thou so soon forgotten the nymph of the fountain? Has one song, idly piped in thine ear, been sufficient to charm away the cherished tenderness of a whole summer?"

The wise may smile -- but I am in a confiding mood, and must confess my weakness. I felt a degree of compunction at this sudden infidelity, yet I could not resist the power of present fascination. My peace of mind was destroyed by conflicting claims. The nymph of the fountain came over my memory, with all the associations of fairy footsteps, shady groves, soft echoes, and wild streamlets; but this new passion was produced by a strain of soul-subduing melody, still lingering in my ear, aided by a downy bed, fragrant flowers, and rose-colored curtains. "Unhappy youth!" sighed I to myself, "distracted by such rival passions, and the empire of thy heart thus violently contested by the sound of a voice, and the print of a footstep!"

I had not remained long in this mood, when I heard the door of the room gently opened. I turned my head to see what inhabitant of this enchanted palace should appear; whether page in green, a hideous dwarf, or haggard fairy. It was my own man Scipio. He advanced with cautious step, and was delighted, as he said, to find me so much myself again. My first questions were as to where I was and how I came there? Scipio told me a long story of his having been fishing in a canoe at the time of my hare-brained cruise; of his noticing the gathering squall, and my impending danger; of his hastening to join me, but arriving just in time to snatch me from a watery grave; of the great difficulty in restoring me to animation; and of my being subsequently conveyed, in a state of insensibility, to this mansion.

"But where am I?" was the reiterated demand.

"In the house of Mr. Somerville."

"Somerville -- Somerville!" I recollected to have heard that a gentleman of that name had recently taken up his residence at some distance from my father's abode, on the opposite side of the Hudson. He was commonly known by the name of "French Somerville," from having passed part of his early life in France, and from his exhibiting traces of French taste in his mode of living, and the arrangements of his house. In fact, it was in his pleasure-boat, which had got adrift, that I had made my fanciful and disastrous cruise. All this was simple, straightforward matter of fact, and threatened to demolish all the cobweb romance I had been spinning, when fortunately I again heard the tinkling of a harp. I raised myself in bed and listened.

"Scipio," said I, with some little hesitation, "I heard some one singing just now. Who was it?"

"Oh, that was Miss Julia."

"Julia! Julia! Delightful! what a name! And, Scipio -- is she -- is she pretty?"

Scipio grinned from ear to ear. "Except Miss Sophy, she was the most beautiful young lady he had ever seen."

I should observe, that my sister Sophia was considered by all the servants a paragon of perfection.

Scipio now offered to remove the basket of flowers; he was afraid their odor might be too powerful; but Miss Julia had given them that morning to be placed in my room.

These flowers, then, had been gathered by the fairy fingers of my unseen beauty; that sweet breath which had filled my ear with melody had passed over them. I made Scipio hand them to me, culled several of the most delicate, and laid them on my bosom.

Mr. Somerville paid me a visit not long afterward. He was an interesting study for me, for he was the father of my unseen beauty, and probably resembled her. I scanned him closely. He was a tall and elegant man, with an open, affable manner, and an erect and graceful carriage. His eyes were bluish-gray, and, though not dark, yet at times were sparkling and expressive. His hair was dressed and powdered, and being lightly combed up from his forehead, added to the loftiness of his aspect. He was fluent in discourse, but his conversation had the quiet tone of polished society, without any of those bold flights of thought, and picturings of fancy, which I so much admired.

My imagination was a little puzzled, at first, to make out of this assemblage of personal and mental qualities a picture that should harmonize with my previous idea of the fair unseen. By dint, however, of selecting what it liked, and giving a touch here and a touch there, it soon furnished out a satisfactory portrait.

"Julia must be tall," thought I, "and of exquisite grace and dignity. She is not quite so courtly as her father, for she has been brought up in the retirement of the country. Neither is she of such vivacious deportment;

for the tones of her voice are soft and plaintive, and she loves pathetic music. She is rather pensive -- yet not too pensive; just what is called interesting. Her eyes are like her father's, except that they are of a purer blue, and more tender and languishing. She has light hair--not exactly flaxen, for I do not like flaxen hair, but between that and auburn. In a word, she is a tall, elegant, imposing, languishing blue-eyed, romantic-looking beauty." And having thus finished her picture, I felt ten times more in love with her than ever.

I felt so much recovered that I would at once have left my room, but Mr. Somerville objected to it. He had sent early word to my family of my safety; and my father arrived in the course of the morning. He was shocked at learning the risk I had run, but rejoiced to find me so much restored, and was warm in his thanks to Mr. Somerville for his kindness. The other only required, in return, that I might remain two or three days as his guest, to give time for my recovery, and for our forming a closer acquaintance; a request which my father readily granted. Scipio accordingly accompanied my father home, and returned with a supply of clothes, and with affectionate letters from my mother and sisters.

The next morning, aided by Scipio, I made my toilet with rather more care than usual, and descended the stairs with some trepidation, eager to see the original of the portrait which had been so completely pictured in my imagination.

On entering the parlor, I found it deserted. Like the rest of the house, it was furnished in a foreign style. The curtains were of French silk; there were Grecian couches, marble tables, pier-glasses, and chandeliers. What chiefly attracted my eye, were documents of female taste that I saw around me; a piano, with an ample stock of Italian music: a book of poetry lying on the sofa; a vase of fresh flowers on a table, and a portfolio open with a skillful and half-finished sketch of them. In the window was a canary bird, in a gilt cage, and near by, the harp that had been in Julia's arms. Happy harp! But where was the being that reigned in this little empire of delicacies?--that breathed poetry and song, and dwelt among birds and flowers, and rose-colored curtains?

Suddenly I heard the hall door fly open, the quick pattering of light steps, a wild, capricious strain of music, and the shrill barking of a dog. A light, frolic nymph of fifteen came tripping into the room, playing on a flageolet, with a little spaniel romping after her. Her gypsy hat had fallen back upon her shoulders; a profusion of glossy brown hair was blown in rich ringlets about her face, which beamed through them with the brightness of smiles and dimples.

At sight of me she stopped short, in the most beautiful confusion, stammered out a word or two about looking for her father, glided out of the door, and I heard her bounding up the staircase, like a frightened fawn, with the little dog barking after her.

When Miss Somerville returned to the parlor, she was quite a different being. She entered, stealing along by her mother's side with noiseless step, and sweet timidity; her hair was prettily adjusted, and a soft blush mantled on her damask cheek. Mr. Somerville accompanied the ladies, and introduced me regularly to them. There were many kind inquiries and much sympathy expressed, on the subject of my nautical accident, and some remarks upon the wild scenery of the neighborhood, with which the ladies seemed perfectly acquainted.

"You must know," said Mr. Somerville, "that we are great navigators, and delight in exploring every nook and corner of the river. My daughter, too, is a great hunter of the picturesque, and transfers every rock and glen to her portfolio. By the way, my dear, show Mr. Mountjoy that pretty scene you have lately sketched." Julia complied, blushing, and drew from her portfolio a colored sketch. I almost started at the sight. It was my favorite brook. A sudden thought darted across my mind. I glanced down my eye, and beheld the divinest little foot in the world. Oh, blissful conviction! The struggle of my affections was at an end. The voice and the footstep were no longer at variance. Julia Somerville was the nymph of the fountain!

What conversation passed during breakfast I do not recollect, and hardly was conscious of at the time, for my thoughts were in complete confusion. I wished to gaze on Miss Somerville, but did not dare. Once, indeed, I ventured a glance. She was at that moment darting a similar one from under a covert of ringlets. Our eyes seemed shocked by the rencontre, and fell; hers through the natural modesty of her sex, mine through a bashfulness produced by the previous workings of my imagination. That glance, however, went like a sunbeam to my heart.

A convenient mirror favored my diffidence, and gave me the reflection of Miss Somerville's form. It is true it only presented the back of her head, but she had the merit of an ancient statue; contemplate her from any point of view, she was beautiful. And yet she was totally different from everything I had before conceived of beauty. She was not the serene, meditative maid that I had pictured the nymph of the fountain; nor the tall, soft, languishing, blue-eyed, dignified being that I had fancied the minstrel of the harp. There was nothing of dignity about her: she was girlish in her appearance, and scarcely of the middle size; but then there was the tenderness of budding youth; the sweetness of the half-blown rose, when not a tint of perfume has been withered or exhaled; there were smiles and dimples, and all the soft witcheries of ever-varying expression. I wondered that I could ever have admired any other style of beauty.

After breakfast, Mr. Somerville departed to attend to the concerns of his estate, and gave me in charge of the ladies. Mrs. Somerville also was called away by her household cares, and I was left alone with Julia! Here, then, was the situation which of all others I had most coveted. I was in the presence of the lovely being that had so long been the desire of my heart. We were alone; propitious opportunity for a lover! Did I seize upon it? Did I break out in one of my accustomed rhapsodies? No such thing! Never was being more awkwardly embarrassed.

"What can be the cause of this?" thought I. "Surely, I cannot stand in awe of this young girl. I am of course her superior in intellect, and am never embarrassed in company with my tutor, notwithstanding all his wisdom."

It was passing strange. I felt that if she were an old woman, I should be quite at my ease; if she were even an ugly woman, I should make out very well: it was her beauty that overpowered me. How little do lovely women know what awful beings they are, in the eyes of inexperienced youth! Young men brought up in the fashionable circles of our cities will smile at all this. Accustomed to mingle incessantly in female society, and to have the romance of the heart deadened by a thousand frivolous flirtations, women are nothing but women in their eyes; but to a susceptible youth like myself, brought up in the country, they are perfect divinities.

Miss Somerville was at first a little embarrassed herself; but, somehow or other, women have a natural adroitness in recovering their self-possession; they are more alert in their minds, and graceful in their manners. Besides, I was but an ordinary personage in Miss Somerville's eyes; she was not under the influence of such a singular course of imaginings as had surrounded her, in my eyes, with the illusions of romance. Perhaps, too, she saw the confusion in the opposite camp and gained courage from the discovery. At any rate she was the first to take the field.

Her conversation, however, was only on commonplace topics, and in an easy, well-bred style. I endeavored to respond in the same manner; but I was strangely incompetent to the task. My ideas were frozen up; even words seemed to fail me. I was excessively vexed at myself, for I wished to be uncommonly elegant. I tried two or three times to turn a pretty thought, or to utter a fine sentiment; but it would come forth so trite, so forced, so mawkish, that I was ashamed of it. My very voice sounded discordantly, though I sought to modulate it into the softest tones. "The truth is," thought I to myself, "I cannot bring my mind down to the small talk necessary for young girls; it is too masculine and robust for the mincing measure of parlor gossip. I am a philosopher -- and that accounts for it."

The entrance of Mrs. Somerville at length gave me relief. I at once breathed freely, and felt a vast deal of confidence come over me. "This is strange," thought I, "that the appearance of another woman should revive my courage; that I should be a better match for two women than one. However, since it is so, I will take advantage of the circumstance, and let this young lady see that I am not so great a simpleton as she probably thinks me."

I accordingly took up the book of poetry which lay upon the sofa. It was Milton's Paradise Lost. Nothing could have been more fortunate; it afforded a fine scope for my favorite vein of grandiloquence. I went largely into a discussion of its merits, or rather an enthusiastic eulogy of them. My observations were addressed to Mrs. Somerville, for I found I could talk to her with more ease than to her daughter. She appeared alive to the beauties of the poet and disposed to meet me in the discussion; but it was not my object to hear her talk; it was to talk myself. I anticipated all she had to say, overpowered her with the copiousness of my ideas, and supported and illustrated them by long citations from the author.

While thus holding forth, I cast a side glance to see how Miss Somerville was affected. She had some embroidery stretched on a frame before her, but had paused in her labor, and was looking down as if lost in mute attention. I felt a glow of self-satisfaction, but I recollected, at the same time, with a kind of pique, the advantage she had enjoyed over me in our tete-a-tete. I determined to push my triumph, and accordingly kept on with redoubled ardor, until I had fairly exhausted my subject, or rather my thoughts.

I had scarce come to a full stop, when Miss Somerville raised her eyes from the work on which they had been fixed, and turning to her mother, observed: "I have been considering, mamma, whether to work these flowers plain, or in colors."

Had an ice-bolt shot to my heart, it could not have chilled me more effectually. "What a fool," thought I, "have I been making myself -- squandering away fine thoughts, and fine language, upon a light mind and an ignorant ear! This girl knows nothing of poetry. She has no soul, I fear, for its beauties. Can any one have real sensibility of heart, and not be alive to poetry? However, she is young; this part of her education has been neglected; there is time enough to remedy it. I will be her preceptor. I will kindle in her mind the sacred flame, and lead her through the fairy land of song. But after all, it is rather unfortunate that I should have fallen in love with a woman who knows nothing of poetry."

I passed a day not altogether satisfactory. I was a little disappointed that Miss Somerville did not show more poetical feeling. "I am afraid, after all," said I to myself, "she is light and girlish, and more fitted to pluck wild flowers, play on the flageolet, and romp with little dogs than to converse with a man of my turn."

I believe, however, to tell the truth, I was more out of humor with myself. I thought I had made the worst first appearance that ever hero made, either in novel or fairy tale. I was out of all patience, when I called to mind my awkward attempts at ease and elegance, in the tete-a-tete. And then my intolerable long lecture about poetry to catch the applause of a heedless auditor! But there I was not to blame. I had certainly been eloquent: it was her fault that the eloquence was wasted. To meditate upon the embroidery of a flower, when I was expatiating on the beauties of Milton! She might at least have admired the poetry, if she did not relish the manner in which it was delivered: though that was not despicable, for I had recited passages in my best style, which my mother and sisters had always considered equal to a play. "Oh, it is evident," thought I, "Miss Somerville has very little soul!"

Such were my fancies and cogitations during the day, the greater part of which was spent in my chamber, for I was still languid. My evening was passed in the drawing-room, where I overlooked Miss Somerville's portfolio of sketches. They were executed with great taste, and showed a nice observation of the peculiarities of nature. They were all her own, and free from those cunning tints and touches of the drawing-master, by which young ladies' drawings, like their heads, are dressed up for company. There was no garish and vulgar trick of colors, either; all was executed with singular truth and simplicity.

"And yet," thought I, "this little being, who has so pure an eye to take in, as in a limpid brook, all the graceful forms and magic tints of nature, has no soul for poetry!"

Mr. Somerville, toward the latter part of the evening, observing my eye to wander occasionally to the harp, interpreted and met my wishes with his accustomed civility.

"Julia, my dear," said he, "Mr. Mountjoy would like to hear a little music from your harp; let us hear, too, the sound of your voice."

Julia immediately complied, without any of that hesitation and difficulty, by which young ladies are apt to make company pay dear for bad music. She sang a sprightly strain, in a brilliant style, that came trilling playfully over the ear; and the bright eye and dimpling smile showed that her little heart danced with the song. Her pet canary bird, who hung close by, was awakened by the music, and burst forth into an emulating strain. Julia smiled with a pretty air of defiance, and played louder.

After some time the music changed, and ran into a plaintive strain, in a minor key. Then it was that all the former witchery of her voice came over me; then it was that she seemed to sing from the heart and to the heart. Her fingers moved about the chords as if they scarcely touched them. Her whole manner and appearance changed; her eyes beamed with the softest expression; her countenance, her frame, all seemed subdued into tenderness. She rose from the harp, leaving it still vibrating with sweet sounds, and moved toward her father, to bid him good-night.

His eyes had been fixed on her intently during her performance. As she came before him he parted her shining ringlets with both his hands, and looked down with the fondness of a father on her innocent face. The music seemed still lingering in its lineaments, and the action of her father brought a moist gleam in her eye. He kissed her fair forehead, after the French mode of parental caressing: "Goodnight, and God bless you," said he, "my good little girl!"

Julia tripped away, with a tear in her eye, a dimple in her cheek, and a light heart in her bosom. I thought it the prettiest picture of paternal and filial affection I had ever seen.

When I retired to bed, a new train of thoughts crowded into my brain. "After all," said I to myself, "it is clear this girl has a soul, though she was not moved by my eloquence. She has all the outward signs and evidences of poetic feeling. She paints well, and has an eye for nature. She is a fine musician, and enters into the very soul of song. What a pity that she knows nothing of poetry! But we will see what is to be done? I am irretrievably in love with her; what then am I to do? Come down to the level of her mind, or endeavor to raise her to some kind of intellectual equality with myself? That is the most generous course. She will look up to me as a benefactor. I shall become associated in her mind with the lofty thoughts and harmonious graces of poetry. She is apparently docile: besides the difference of our ages will give me an ascendency over her. She cannot be above sixteen years of age, and I am full turned to twenty." So, having built this most delectable of air castles, I fell asleep.

The next morning I was quite a different being. I no longer felt fearful of stealing a glance at Julia; on the contrary, I contemplated her steadily, with the benignant eye of a benefactor. Shortly after breakfast I found myself alone with her, as I had on the preceding morning; but I felt nothing of the awkwardness of our previous tete-a-tete. I was elevated by the consciousness of my intellectual superiority and should almost have felt a sentiment of pity for the ignorance of the lovely little being, if I had not felt also the assurance that I should be able to dispel it. "But it is time," thought I, "to open school." Julia was occupied in arranging some music on her piano. I looked over two or three songs; they were Moore's Irish melodies.

"These are pretty things!" said I, flirting the leaves over lightly, and giving a slight shrug, by way of qualifying the opinion.

"Oh, I love them of all things," said Julia, "they're so touching!"

"Then you like them for the poetry," said I, with an encouraging smile.

"Oh, yes; she thought them charmingly written."

Now was my time. "Poetry," said I, assuming a didactic attitude and air, "poetry is one of the most pleasing studies that can occupy a youthful mind. It renders us susceptible of the gentle impulses of humanity, and cherishes a delicate perception of all that is virtuous and elevated in morals, and graceful and beautiful in physics. It --"

I was going on in a style that would have graced a professor of rhetoric, when I saw a light smile playing about Miss Somerville's mouth, and that she began to turn over the leaves of a music-book. I recollected her inattention to my discourse of the preceding morning. "There is no fixing her light mind," thought I, "by abstract theory; we will proceed practically." As it happened, the identical volume of Milton's Paradise Lost was lying at hand.

"Let me recommend to you, my young friend," said I, in one of those tones of persuasive admonition, which I had so often loved in Glencoe, "let me recommend to you this admirable poem; you will find in it sources of intellectual enjoyment far superior to those songs which have delighted you." Julia looked at the book, and then at me, with a whimsically dubious air. "Milton's Paradise Lost?" said she; "oh, I know the greater part of that by heart."

I had not expected to find my pupil so far advanced; however, the Paradise Lost is a kind of school book, and its finest passages are given to young ladies as tasks.

"I find," said I to myself, "I must not treat her as so complete a novice; her inattention yesterday could not have proceeded from absolute ignorance, but merely from a want of poetic feeling. I'll try her again."

I now determined to dazzle her with my own erudition, and launched into a harangue that would have done honor to an institute. Pope, Spenser, Chaucer, and the old dramatic writers were all dipped into, with the excursive flight of a swallow. I did not confine myself to English poets, but gave a glance at the French and Italian schools; I passed over Ariosto in full wing, but paused on Tasso's Jerusalem Delivered. I dwelt on the character of Clorinda: "There's a character," said I, "that you will find well worthy a woman's study. It shows to what exalted heights of heroism the sex can rise, how gloriously they may share even in the stern concerns of men."

"For my part," said Julia, gently taking advantage of a pause, "for my part, I prefer the character of Sophronia."

I was thunderstruck. She then had read Tasso! This girl that I had been treating as an ignoramus in poetry! She proceeded with a slight glow of the cheek, summoned up perhaps by a casual glow of feeling:

"I do not admire those masculine heroines," said she, "who aim at the bold qualities of the opposite sex. Now Sophronia only exhibits the real qualities of a woman, wrought up to their highest excitement. She is modest, gentle, and retiring, as it becomes a woman to be; but she has all the strength of affection proper to a woman. She cannot fight for her people as Clorinda does, but she can offer herself up, and die to serve them. You may admire Clorinda, but you surely would be more apt to love Sophronia; at least," added she, suddenly appearing to recollect herself, and blushing at having launched into such a discussion, "at least that is what papa observed when we read the poem together."

"Indeed," said I, dryly, for I felt disconcerted and nettled at being unexpectedly lectured by my pupil; "indeed, I do not exactly recollect the passage."

"Oh," said Julia, "I can repeat it to you;" and she immediately gave it in Italian.

Heavens and earth! -- here was a situation! I knew no more of Italian than I did of the language of Psalmanazar. What a dilemma for a would-be-wise man to be placed in! I saw Julia waited for my opinion.

"In fact," said I, hesitating, "I -- I do not exactly understand Italian."

"Oh," said Julia, with the utmost naivete, "I have no doubt it is very beautiful in the translation."

I was glad to break up school, and get back to my chamber, full of the mortification which a wise man in love experiences on finding his mistress wiser than himself. "Translation! translation!" muttered I to myself, as I jerked the door shut behind me: "I am surprised my father has never had me instructed in the modern languages. They are all important. What is the use of Latin and Greek? No one speaks them; but here, the moment I make my appearance in the world, a little girl slaps Italian in my face. However, thank heaven, a language is easily learned. The moment I return home, I'll set about studying Italian; and to prevent future surprise, I will study Spanish and German at the same time; and if any young lady attempts to quote Italian upon me again, I'll bury her under a heap of High Dutch poetry!"

I felt now like some mighty chieftain, who has carried the war into a weak country, with full confidence of success, and been repulsed and obliged to draw off his forces from before some inconsiderable fortress.

"However," thought I, "I have as yet brought only my light artillery into action; we shall see what is to be done with my heavy ordnance. Julia is evidently well versed in poetry; but it is natural she should be so; it is allied to painting and music, and is congenial to the light graces of the female character. We will try her on graver themes."

I felt all my pride awakened; it even for a time swelled higher than my love. I was determined completely to establish my mental superiority, and subdue the intellect of this little being; it would then be time to sway the scepter of gentle empire, and win the affections of her heart.

Accordingly, at dinner I again took the field, en potence. I now addressed myself to Mr. Somerville, for I was about to enter upon topics in which a young girl like her could not be well versed. I led, or rather forced, the conversation into a vein of historical erudition, discussing several of the most prominent facts of ancient history, and accompanying them with sound, indisputable apothegms.

Mr. Somerville listened to me with the air of a man receiving information. I was encouraged, and went on gloriously from theme to theme of school declamation. I sat with Marius on the ruins of Carthage; I defended the bridge with Horatius Cocles; thrust my hand into the flame with Martius Scaevola, and plunged with Curtius into the yawning gulf; I fought side by side with Leonidas, at the straits of Thermopylae; and was going full drive into the battle of Plataea, when my memory, which is the worst in the world, failed me, just as I wanted the name of the Lacedemonian commander.

"Julia, my dear," said Mr. Somerville, "perhaps you may recollect the name of which Mr. Mountjoy is in quest?"

Julia colored slightly. "I believe," said she, in a low voice, "I believe it was Pausanius."

This unexpected sally, instead of re-enforcing me, threw my whole scheme of battle into confusion, and the Athenians remained unmolested in the field.

I am half inclined, since, to think Mr. Somerville meant this as a sly hit at my schoolboy pedantry; but he was too well bred not to seek to relieve me from my mortification. "Oh!" said he, "Julia is our family book of reference for names, dates, and distances, and has an excellent memory for history and geography."

I now became desperate; as a last resource I turned to metaphysics. "If she is a philosopher in petticoats," thought I, "it is all over with me." Here, however, I had the field to myself. I gave chapter and verse of my tutor's lectures, heightened by all his poetical illustrations; I even went further than he had ever ventured, and plunged into such depths of metaphysics that I was in danger of sticking in the mire at the bottom. Fortunately, I had auditors who apparently could not detect my flounderings. Neither Mr. Somerville nor his daughter offered the least interruption.

When the ladies had retired, Mr. Somerville sat some time with me; and as I was no longer anxious to astonish, I permitted myself to listen, and found that he was really agreeable. He was quite communicative, and from his conversation I was enabled to form a juster idea of his daughter's character, and the mode in which she had been brought up. Mr. Somerville had mingled much with the world, and with what is termed fashionable society. He had experienced its cold elegances and gay insincerities; its dissipation of the spirits and squanderings of the heart. Like many men of the world, though he had wandered too far from nature ever to return to it, yet he had the good taste and good feeling to look back fondly to its simple delights, and to determine that his child, if possible, should never leave them. He had superintended her education with scrupulous care, storing her mind with the graces of polite literature, and with such knowledge as would enable it to furnish its own amusement and occupation, and giving her all the accomplishments that sweeten and enliven the circle of domestic life. He had been particularly sedulous to exclude all fashionable affectations; all false sentiment, false sensibility, and false romance. "Whatever advantages she may possess," said he, "she is quite unconscious of them. She is a capricious little being, in everything but her affections; she is, however, free from art; simple, ingenuous, amiable, and, I thank God! happy."

Such was the eulogy of a fond father, delivered with a tenderness that touched me. I could not help making a casual inquiry, whether, among the graces of polite literature, he had included a slight tincture of metaphysics. He smiled, and told me he had not.

On the whole, when, as usual, that night, I summed up the day's observations on my pillow, I was not altogether dissatisfied. "Miss Somerville," said I, "loves poetry, and I like her the better for it. She has the advantage of me in Italian; agreed; what is it to know a variety of languages, but merely to have a variety of sounds to express the same idea? Original thought is the ore of the mind; language is but the accidental stamp and coinage by which it is put into circulation. If I can furnish an original idea, what care I how many languages she can translate it into? She may be able also to quote names and dates and latitudes better than I; but that is a mere effort of the memory. I admit she is more accurate in history and geography than I; but then she knows nothing of metaphysics."

I had now sufficiently recovered to return home; yet I could not think of leaving Mr. Somerville's without having a little further conversation with him on the subject of his daughter's education.

"This Mr. Somerville," thought I, "is a very accomplished, elegant man; he has seen a good deal of the world, and, upon the whole, has profited by what he has seen. He is not without information, and, as far as he thinks, appears to think correctly; but, after all, he is rather superficial, and does not think profoundly. He seems to take no delight in those metaphysical abstractions that are the proper aliment of masculine minds. I called to mind various occasions in which I had indulged largely in metaphysical discussions, but could recollect no instance where I had been able to draw him out. He had listened, it is true, with attention, and smiled as if in acquiescence, but had always appeared to avoid reply. Besides, I had made several sad blunders in the glow of eloquent declamation; but he had never interrupted me, to notice and correct them, as he would have done had he been versed in the theme.

"Now, it is really a great pity," resumed I, "that he should have the entire management of Miss Somerville's education. What a vast advantage it would be if she could be put for a little time under the superintendence

of Glencoe. He would throw some deeper shades of thought into her mind, which at present is all sunshine; not but that Mr. Somerville has done very well, as far as he has gone; but then he has merely prepared the soil for the strong plants of useful knowledge. She is well versed in the leading facts of history, and the general course of belles-lettres," said I; "a little more philosophy would do wonders."

I accordingly took occasion to ask Mr. Somerville for a few moments' conversation in his study, the morning I was to depart. When we were alone I opened the matter fully to him. I commenced with the warmest eulogium of Glencoe's powers of mind and vast acquirements, and ascribed to him all my proficiency in the higher branches of knowledge. I begged, therefore, to recommend him as a friend calculated to direct the studies of Miss Somerville; to lead her mind, by degrees, to the contemplation of abstract principles, and to produce habits of philosophical analysis; "which," added I, gently smiling, "are not often cultivated by young ladies." I ventured to hint, in addition, that he would find Mr. Glencoe a most valuable and interesting acquaintance for himself; one who would stimulate and evolve the powers of his mind; and who might open to him tracts of inquiry and speculation to which perhaps he had hitherto been a stranger.

Mr. Somerville listened with grave attention. When I had finished, he thanked me in the politest manner for the interest I took in the welfare of his daughter and himself. He observed that, as it regarded himself, he was afraid he was too old to benefit by the instruction of Mr. Glencoe, and that as to his daughter, he was afraid her mind was but little fitted for the study of metaphysics. "I do not wish," continued he, "to strain her intellects with subjects they cannot grasp, but to make her familiarly acquainted with those that are within the limits of her capacity. I do not pretend to prescribe the boundaries of female genius, and am far from indulging the vulgar opinion that women are unfitted by nature for the highest intellectual pursuits. I speak only with reference to my daughter's tastes and talents. She will never make a learned woman; nor, in truth, do I desire it; for such is the jealousy of our sex, as to mental as well as physical ascendency, that a learned woman is not always the happiest. I do not wish my daughter to excite envy, or to battle with the prejudices of the world; but to glide peaceably through life, on the good will and kind opinions of her friends. She has ample employment for her little head, in the course I have marked out for her; and is busy at present with some branches of natural history, calculated to awaken her perceptions to the beauties and wonders of nature, and to the inexhaustible volume of wisdom constantly spread open before her eyes. I consider that woman most likely to make an agreeable companion, who can draw topics of pleasing remark from every natural object; and most likely to be cheerful and contented, who is continually sensible of the order, the harmony, and the invariable beneficence that reign throughout the beautiful world we inhabit."

"But," added he, smiling, "I am betraying myself into a lecture, instead of merely giving a reply to your kind offer. Permit me to take the liberty, in return, of inquiring a little about your own pursuits. You speak of having finished your education; but of course you have a line of private study and mental occupation marked out; for you must know the importance, both in point of interest and happiness, of keeping the mind employed. May I ask what system you observe in your intellectual exercises?"

"Oh, as to system," I observed, "I could never bring myself into anything of the kind. I thought it best to let my genius take it own course, as it always acted the most vigorously when stimulated by inclination."

Mr. Somerville shook his head. "This same genius," said he, "is a wild quality that runs away with our most promising young men. It has become so much the fashion, too, to give it the reins that it is now thought an animal of too noble and generous a nature to be brought to harness. But it is all a mistake. Nature never designed these high endowments to run riot through society, and throw the whole system into confusion. No, my dear sir, genius, unless it acts upon system, is very apt to be a useless quality to society; sometimes an injurious, and certainly a very uncomfortable one, to its possessor. I have had many opportunities of seeing the progress through life of young men who were accounted geniuses, and have found it too often end in early exhaustion and bitter disappointment; and have as often noticed that these effects might be traced to a total want of system. There were no habits of business, of steady purpose, and regular application, superinduced upon the mind; everything was left to chance and impulse, and native luxuriance, and everything of course ran to waste and wild entanglement. Excuse me if I am tedious on this point, for I feel solicitous to impress it upon you, being an error extremely prevalent in our country and one into which too many of our youth have fallen. I am happy, however, to observe the zeal which still appears to actuate you for the acquisition of knowledge, and augur every good from the elevated bent of your ambition. May I ask what has been your course of study for the last six months?"

Never was question more unluckily timed. For the last six months I had been absolutely buried in novels and romances. Mr. Somerville perceived that the question was embarrassing, and, with his invariable good breeding, immediately resumed the conversation, without waiting for a reply. He took care, however, to turn it in such a way as to draw from me an account of the whole manner in which I had been educated, and the various currents of reading into which my mind had run. He then went on to discuss, briefly but impressively, the different branches of knowledge most important to a young man in my situation; and to my surprise I found him a complete master of those studies on which I had supposed him ignorant, and on which I had been descanting so confidently.

He complimented me, however, very graciously, upon the progress I had made, but advised me for the present to turn my attention to the physical rather than the moral sciences. "These studies," said he, "store a man's mind with valuable facts, and at the same time repress self-confidence, by letting him know how boundless are the realms of knowledge, and how little we can possibly know. Whereas metaphysical studies, though of an ingenious order of intellectual employment, are apt to bewilder some minds with vague speculations. They never know how far they have advanced, or what may be the correctness of their favorite theory. They render many of our young men verbose and declamatory, and prone to mistake the aberrations of their fancy for the inspirations of divine philosophy."

I could not but interrupt him, to assent to the truth of these remarks, and to say that it had been my lot, in the course of my limited experience, to encounter young men of the kind, who had overwhelmed me by their verbosity.

Mr. Somerville smiled. "I trust," said he, kindly, "that you will guard against these errors. Avoid the eagerness with which a young man is apt to hurry into conversation, and to utter the crude and ill-digested notions which he has picked up in his recent studies. Be assured that extensive and accurate knowledge is the slow acquisition of a studious lifetime; that a young man, however pregnant his wit, and prompt his talent, can have mastered but the rudiments of learning, and, in a manner, attained the implements of study. Whatever may have been your past assiduity, you must be sensible that as yet you have but reached the threshold of true knowledge; but at the same time you have the advantage that you are still very young, and have ample time to learn."

Here our conference ended. I walked out of the study a very different being from what I was on entering it. I had gone in with the air of a professor about to deliver a lecture; I came out like a student who had failed in his examination, and been degraded in his class.

"Very young," and "on the threshold of knowledge!" This was extremely flattering to one who had considererd himself an accomplished scholar and a profound philosopher.

"It is singular," thought I; "there seems to have been a spell upon my faculties, ever since I have been in this house. I certainly have not been able to do myself justice. Whenever I have undertaken to advise, I have had the tables turned upon me. It must be that I am strange and diffident among people I am not accustomed to. I wish they could hear me talk at home!"

"After all," added I, on further reflection, "after all there is a great deal of force in what Mr. Somerville has said. Somehow or other, these men of the world do now and then hit upon remarks that would do credit to a philosopher. Some of his general observations came so home that I almost thought they were meant for myself. His advice about adopting a system of study is very judicious. I will immediately put it hi practice. My mind shall operate henceforward with the regularity of clock-work."

How far I succeeded in adopting this plan, how I fared in the further pursuit of knowledge, and how I succeeded in my suit to Julia Somerville, may afford matter for a further communication to the public, if this simple record of my early life is fortunate enough to excite any curiosity.

※※※

**More books about New York from
New York History Review**

Ontario Breeze by Phebe White
Plank Road Explorer by Henry Marvin
Queen City Adventure by Emma Latier
Home in These Hills by Viola Coolbaugh
In Their Honor by Diane Janowski
My Centennial Diary by Earll Gurnee
A Darned Good Time by Miss Lucy Potter

NewYorkHistoryReview.com

www.ingramcontent.com/pod-product-compliance
Lightning Source LLC
Chambersburg PA
CBHW021129130626
46554CB00002B/925